EYEWITNESS
MYTHOLOGY

Māori ceremonial adze (axe)

Monstrous Chimera of ancient Greek mythology

Medusa, a hideous Greek gorgon

Ritual sword used in Ogun worship, west Africa

The Wealthy One (1988), a contemporary Native American mask

Hindu animal god Garuda

Mould and casting of Venus, Roman goddess of love

Tibetan *vajras*
representing
thunderbolts
of the gods

EYEWITNESS
MYTHOLOGY

Written by
NEIL PHILIP

Māori bird-man kite

Native
American
shaman

DK

豊川閣霊験守護攸

Japanese
prayer
offerings

African fortune-telling
cowrie shells

Tangaroa, supreme god of Polynesia

DK Penguin
Random
House

Project editor Melanie Halton
Art editor Joanne Connor
Senior managing editor Linda Martin
Senior managing art editor Julia Harris
Production Kate Oliver
Picture research Andy Sansom
DTP designer Andrew O'Brien

THIRD EDITION
Editors Clare Hibbert, Steve Setford, Jessamy Wood
Art editors Rebecca Johns, Peter Radcliffde
Senior editor Shalia Awan
Managing editors Linda Esposito, Julie Ferris, Jane Yorke
Managing art editors Owen Peyton Jones, Jane Thomas
Art directors Simon Webb, Martin Wilson
Associate publisher Andrew Macintyre
Picture researchers Carolyn Clerkin, Harriet Mills
Production editors Jenny Jacoby, Hitesh Patel, Marc Staples
DTP designer Siu Yin Ho
Jacket editor Adam Powley
Editorial consultant Neil Philip

RELAUNCH EDITION

DK DELHI
Project Editor Priyanka Kharbanda
Project Art Editor Neha Sharma
Assistant Editor Antara Raghavan
Assistant Art Editor Priyanka Bansal
DTP Designer Pawan Kumar
Senior DTP Designer Harish Aggarwal
Picture Researcher Sakshi Saluja
Jacket Designer Juhi Sheth
Managing Editor Kingshuk Ghoshal
Managing Art Editor Govind Mittal

DK LONDON
Senior Art Editor Spencer Holbrook
Editor Anna Streiffert Limerick
Jacket Editor Claire Gell
Jacket Design Development Manager Sophia MTT
Producer, pre-production Gillian Reid
Producer Gary Batchelor
Managing Editor Francesca Baines
Managing Art Editor Philip Letsu
Publisher Andrew Macintyre
Associate Publishing Director Liz Wheeler
Art Director Karen Self
Design Director Philip Ormerod
Publishing Director Jonathan Metcalf

This Eyewitness ® Guide has been conceived by
Dorling Kindersley Limited and Editions Gallimard

This edition published in 2017
First published in Great Britain in 1990 by
Dorling Kindersley Limited
80 Strand, London, WC2R 0RL

Copyright © 1999, 2004, 2011, 2017 Dorling Kindersley Limited
A Penguin Random House Company
10 9 8 7 6 5 4 3 2 1
001 – 305104 – June/2017

A CIP catalogue record for this book is available from the British Library.
ISBN 978-0-2412-9718-6

Printed and bound in China

A WORLD OF IDEAS:
SEE ALL THERE IS TO KNOW

www.dk.com

Oceanic
ceremonial axe

Staff representin
African thunder g
Shango's axe

Back of
Tangaroa

Contents

Native American Navajo
sand-painting

Mythology 6

Creation of the world 8

The cosmos 10

Sun and Moon 12

Humankind 14

Supreme beings 16

Floods and storms 18

The elements 20

The natural world 22

Fertility and birth 24

Children of gods 26

Ancestor worship 28

Evil forces 30

Superheroes 32

Journeys and quests 34

Divine weapons 36

Gods of war 38

Contacting the spirits 40

Love and fortune 42

Tricksters 44

Giants and small folk 46

Animal idols 48

Mythical beasts 50

Shapeshifters 52

Painting the story 54

Universal creatures 56

The afterlife 58

Sacred sites 60

End of the world 62

Did you know? 64

Mythical meanings 66

Find out more 68

Glossary 70

Index 72

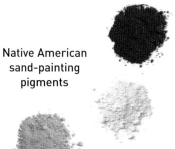

Native American
sand-painting
pigments

Mother Earth
This gold pendant shows Astarte, the Canaanite goddess of fertility. A great mother goddess appears in most mythologies.

Mythology

The word "myth" comes from the Greek *mythos*, meaning a word or story. In daily speech it can be something people believe is not true. But mythology is a collection of stories that help people make sense of the world. Every culture has stories about the creation of Earth, the origins of humankind, and the meaning of life. Mythology puts across religious ideas in stories that explore rather than explain.

Long-haired figures represent the shaman wrestling with the beaver.

Creation of the world
Many mythologies tell how the creator emerged from a cosmic egg or a primordial (existing from the beginning) ocean. The world was then created, perhaps from the creator's own body, from mud, or from the power of words or thought. The first Hindu god, Brahma, is said to have been born from a golden egg floating on the first waters.

Hindu creation symbol

Myth beginnings

The oldest living mythology comes from the Australian Aborigines, whose stories of the sacred Dreamtime stretch back 40,000 years. Myths of diverse cultures are often linked by themes. This timeline shows when societies started shaping their myths.

Burning stick symbolizes the beaver's magical powers

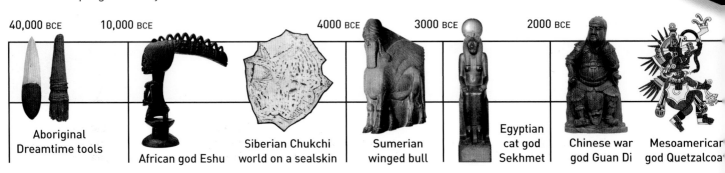

40,000 BCE	10,000 BCE		4000 BCE	3000 BCE		2000 BCE	
Aboriginal Dreamtime tools	African god Eshu	Siberian Chukchi world on a sealskin	Sumerian winged bull	Egyptian cat god Sekhmet		Chinese war god Guan Di	Mesoamerican god Quetzalcoa

Guiding ancestors

Ancestors play a key role in world mythology. For Australian Aborigines, the laws and customs established by ancestor spirits act as guidelines for life today. These ancestors exist outside of time, in the eternal present of the Dreamtime.

Challenging the gods

The Bible tells how Nimrod, king of Babylon, built a tower to reach heaven and make war on God. So God sent 70 angels to confuse the builders' tongues. Some say this is why people now speak different languages.

The Tower of Babel fell when the workmen could no longer understand one another.

Storytelling

This Medicine Beaver mask tells the story of the life-or-death struggle between a shaman, or medicine man, of the North American Nisga'a people and a giant beaver. The shaman made the beaver into his spirit helper.

Persephone and Hades

Many mythologies hope for a new life after death. The ancient Egyptians and Greeks linked the afterlife with the annual death and resurrection of corn. The Greeks worshipped Persephone, daughter of the corn goddess Demeter, as queen of the dead.

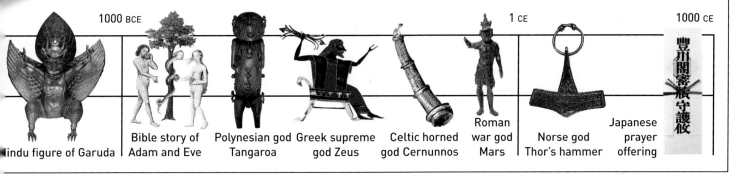

1000 BCE   1 CE   1000 CE

Hindu figure of Garuda | Bible story of Adam and Eve | Polynesian god Tangaroa | Greek supreme god Zeus | Celtic horned god Cernunnos | Roman war god Mars | Norse god Thor's hammer | Japanese prayer offering

Creation of the world

Cosmic egg
A bird-man from Rapa Nui (Easter Island, in the Pacific Ocean) is shown holding the cosmic egg that contains the world.

Many peoples agree that the world was made as an act of creation by a divine being. The earliest myths describe a vast ocean from which the world energed. Nun was god of the ancient Egyptian mythological ocean. The Arctic Tikigaq people say that Raven harpooned a great whale, which floated and became dry land.

Fire and ice
The Vikings believed the world began when fire from the south met ice from the north. Ice began thawing at the centre. The drips shaped into the first being, Ymir, whose sweat formed the frost giants, beings with superhuman strength.

Pottery figurine of Gaia from Thebes, 450 BCE

Out of chaos
The ancient Greeks believed the first to be born from the primeval, or original, chaos was Gaia, or Earth. Gaia was conceived as a floating disc, encircled by the river Oceanus. Gaia gave birth to Uranus (the sky) and Cronos (time).

Ahura Mazda

Big Bang
Scientists now believe the world began with the Big Bang, a huge explosion 13 billion years ago that created the Universe.

Created from goodness
Ancient Persians believed in twin spirits: Ahura Mazda, who was good, and Ahriman, who was evil. Ahura Mazda made the physical world, set time in motion, and created humankind.

Part of the ancient Persian Tree of Life relief, 9th century BCE

Turtle Island

Many Native American tribes believe the world is supported on a turtle's back. The Seneca tribe thought that a toad that lived on the primal waters dived down to fetch mud to place on the turtle's back. This mud became Earth.

The first land was said to have been created on a turtle's back.

19th-century Native American Cheyenne shield

The Milky Way and planets of the Solar System

Curdling ocean

The Japanese god Izanagi and his wife Izanami stood on the Floating Bridge of Heaven and stirred the ocean with a jewelled spear until it curdled and formed the island Onokoro.

Ocean churning

In this creation cycle, the elixir of immortality was missing. Hindu gods churned the ocean with Mount Mandara as a paddle. The sea turned to milk and butter, and the Sun and Moon rose, before the elixir was finally created.

Vishnu sits on Mount Mandara.

Vasuki, the cosmic serpent, was used as a rope to twist the mountain.

The mountain is supported by a giant turtle.

The cosmos

People always question the mysteries of the world, from its origin and shape to its cosmos, or order. The world is often thought to come from a cosmic egg. In China, the warring forces of yin and yang in the egg created the first being, Pan Gu. Africa's Dogon people believe the world came from a vibrating egg opening to reveal a creator spirit. The Ainu of Japan believed in six skies above Earth, and six worlds beneath it. Polynesia's Mangaian people say the Universe is held in a big coconut shell.

Inuit people of the Arctic tundra build igloos, which are round, like the world.

Sealskin

This sealskin painted by the Chukchi people of Siberia shows the Arctic world – Sun, Moon, land, sea, and sky. Humans share creation with spirits, animals, and gods, such as the creator Raven.

Yin and yang

The ancient Chinese believed the first being, Pan Gu, was created in a cosmic egg by the opposing forces of yin and yang. When the conflict between yin and yang broke the egg, Pan Gu was born. After he died, his body formed the land – and his fleas became humankind.

Yin and yang symbolize universal opposites that must be balanced for a harmonious world.

Brahma, the creator of the Universe, is shown on Vishnu's forehead.

Vishnu's conch shell symbolizes the first vibration of the Universe – the sound "om".

The discus symbolizes the mind and the Sun.

World tree

The Vikings of Scandinavia believed there were nine worlds, including humankind's Middle Earth. These were arranged in layers around Yggdrasil, an ash tree at the centre of the cosmos, called the World Tree.

Cosmic stone

This Babylonian boundary stone shows the gods of the cosmos as witnesses to a legal agreement. At the top are symbols of the goddess of love and war, Ishtar; Moon god, Sin; and Sun god, Shamash. A snake from the underworld wriggles up the side.

is represented by a crescent Moon.

This symbol for the planet Venus represents Ishtar, the goddess of love and war.

Vishnu's lotus flower is a symbol of purity.

Nut and Geb

Ancient Egyptians thought that Earth was male, personified by Geb, the Earth god. Geb mated with his sister, Nut, the sky goddess, to produce the stars.

Each night the Sun god, Ra, is swallowed by Nut, to be born again the next morning.

Snakes writhe in the lowest region of the cosmos, Tala, where murderers are reborn.

Watchful eyes of the owl Koururu, sacrificed by Rongo, god of agriculture, to protect his house

Varuna, god of the waters, sits on an imaginary beast.

This wood carving stood at the entrance to a Māori assembly house on North Island, New Zealand

Papa and Rangi

The Māori of New Zealand tell how Papa, the Earth goddess, coupled with Rangi, the sky god. They clung together so closely that their children could not leave the Earth womb. They were forced apart by their son Tane, the forest god.

This golden mace is a symbol of knowledge.

Vishnu's world

Vishnu, the Preserver, is one of three great gods of the Hindu religion. When Vishnu was incarnated as hero Krishna, Krishna's mother looked into her son's mouth and saw the Universe. This 19th-century painting shows Vishnu as the Universe.

Sun and Moon

The Sun and the Moon have been the subjects of many myths. For the Native American Zuni people, Moonlight-Giving Mother and Sun Father are the givers of light and life. The Native American Cherokee say the Sun is female, and tell of her grief when her daughter died. Her tears caused a flood. The Arctic Chukchi tell how a woman married the Sun, but a beetle took her place. When her son sought out his father, the imposter was found. In another myth, a Chukchi woman married the Moon.

Dealer of days

Moon god Thoth ran the ancient Egyptian calendar, which had 12 months of 30 days. Sky goddess Nut was cursed never to give birth, but won five days to have children.

Roman goddess Diana

Diana, Artemis in Greek mythology, is shown here with her foot on the Moon, with which she was closely associated. More often, however, she is depicted with a crescent Moon in her hair.

The goddess Diana, with one foot on the Moon

The face on this Inuit mask represents the spirit of the Moon.

Decorative feathers represent the stars.

The white border around the face symbolizes the air.

Painted Moon face sculpted in wood

Native American Haida mask

Feeding humankind

Inuit people of the Arctic have a Moon Man called Igaluk or Tarqeq. Shamans (medicine men) make spirit journeys to ask him to ensure that he will send animals for men to hunt.

Polluting the world

A Native American Haida myth tells how Wultcixaiya, son of the Moon, rescued his sister from her unhappy marriage to Pestilence. He broke into their house, freeing his sister, but also polluted the world with sickness.

Sun god Ra

The falcon-headed god Horus joined with Egyptian Sun god Ra and became Ra-Horakhty. He sailed a boat across the sky by day and into the underworld by night.

The Sun's rays beam down on a worshipper.

Pre-Columbian gold Sun mask, 300 BCE

Inca Inti

Viracocha, the creator god of the Incas of Peru, ordered the Sun, Moon, and stars to emerge from the Island of the Sun, in Lake Titicaca, to bring light to the world. Inti, the Sun god, was seen as father of the Sapa Incas (Inca emperors).

Projections symbolize the Sun's rays.

Children of the Sun

Asdiwal, hunter hero of the Native American Tsimshian people, pursued a bear into the sky. The bear was the Sun's daughter, whom Asdiwal married. The Sun's son was a prince of the sky.

Tsimshian chief's ceremonial headdress representing the Sun

Fertility goddess Ishtar

Ea, the water god

Shamash rising between two mountains

Amaterasu holds the imperial sword and necklace.

Enemy of darkness

Babylonian Sun god Shamash was the only being able to cross the ocean of death, until Gilgamesh did so. Shamash was the enemy of darkness.

Sun goddess Amaterasu

Japanese Sun goddess Amaterasu took offence at her brother's jokes, so she hid in a cave, temporarily depriving the world of the Sun.

Humankind

All mythologies tell how the first humans were made. Often the creator shaped them from clay or mud. The Unalit (North Alaskan Inuit) say the first man was born from the pod of a beach pea. Ancient Egyptians believed the first humans were made from the Sun god's tears. For Serbians, people came from the creator's sweat, while Norse god Odin made the first humans from driftwood.

Snake goddess
Nü Wa, the first Chinese goddess, had a girl's face and a snake's body. She was lonely, so she made the first humans from mud and water to cheer herself up.

Brahma has four heads so that he can see in every direction.

Brahma the creator
The Hindu creator Brahma is the universal soul, the Self-Existent Great-Grandfather. He made all the world. He is known as Purusha, First Being. As Purusha, he divided himself into two, male and female, and mated as every creature, from humans to ants.

Tangaroa brings forth other beings.

Carved wooden bowl from west Africa

The cosmic serpent Aido-Hwedo coiled itself around Earth.

Bodies of clay
The west African creator Mawu-Lisa made the first people from clay and water. The man and woman, called Adanhu and Yewa, were sent down from the sky with Rainbow Snake Aido-Hwedo. The first people called out for the god who sent them to Earth.

Adanhu

Yewa

Wooden statue from the Tubuaï Islands in Polynesia, where supreme god Tangaroa is called A'a

Wooden idols

First humans
When the statue of Tangaroa was first discovered, it contained wooden idols like these, which represented the first men and women.

New beings crawl on Tangaroa's back.

Potter's people
The Egyptian ram-god Khnum was the potter who shaped each human and his or her *ka*, or life force, on his potter's wheel. Khnum was worshipped at Elephantine island. An inscription on a block of granite records how prayers to Khnum ended a seven-year famine.

The tree of the knowledge of good and evil

Tangaroa's body cavity contained wooden idols.

Wooden statues
Tangaroa is the Polynesian god of the ocean. In some places, he is the maker of all things. In Tahiti, he is said to have lived in the cosmic egg at the start of time. When he broke out, he created the world, and called forth gods and humans from his body.

Tangaroa creates other gods and humankind from his body.

Adam and Eve
In the Bible, God created Adam, the first man, in his own image. God shaped Adam out of clay and made Eve, the first woman, from one of Adam's ribs.

Supreme beings

One god who rules over all is part of most mythologies. These supreme gods may be associated with the creation of the world and humankind. Many supreme deities, such as Greek god Zeus, are essentially sky gods; others may be Sun, battle, city, or tribal gods. In some African cultures, the supreme god is said to have retired from the world after the creation. Over time, such gods are sometimes almost forgotten.

Thunderbolts were made for Zeus by the Cyclopes, giant helpers in the war against Cronos, Zeus's father.

Ruler of the Greeks
Zeus (known as Jupiter to the Romans) was ruler of the Greek gods. Zeus overthrew his father, Cronos, before establishing his rule. From his many love affairs, he fathered the gods Apollo and Artemis, and heroes Perseus and Heracles.

Made of bronze a... silver, th... Bronze-Age figur... represen... the storn... god Baal.

The Rainmaker
The Canaanite storm god Baal made thunder with his mace and lightning with his lance. Baal revolted against his fath... El by defeating El's favourite, Yam, the sea god.

Babylonian king of the gods
This dog-like dragon is the symbol of Marduk, Babylonian king of the gods. He gained authority over other gods when he agreed to slay the dragon Tiamat. Marduk created humans from the blood of Kingu, Tiamat's son.

Feathered serpent
Half snake, half quetzal bird, Quetzalcoatl was the Aztec lord of life and wind god. He went to the underworld to retrieve the bones of early humans to create new beings.

The feathers of more than 250 quetzal birds make up this headdress.

Aztec serpent god Quetzalcoat...

Quetzal headdress of Montezuma II, the last Aztec ruler

Wooden *kantele* from Karelia in Finland, 1893

Stoneware Taoist shrine of the Ming dynasty, 1406 CE

Lao-tzu, the founder of Taoism, is shown riding a buffalo.

Singing shaman

Väinämöinen, the eternal singer, was the son of Finnish air goddess Ilmatar. He was born old, so no one would marry him. Väinämöinen was a shaman (spiritual guide) whose songs to the sound of his harp-like *kantele* were acts of creative magic.

The Jade Emperor

Lord of the heavens

The Chinese gods formed a huge bureaucracy, led by the Jade Emperor. He was assisted by the God of the Eastern Peak, who had 75 departments under his control, each supervised by lesser gods.

Ebony pestle and mortar from Tanzania, east Africa

Pestle

The God of the Eastern Peak

Mortar

Sky to heaven

Nyame is the sky god of the Ashanti of Africa. He lived with humans until an old woman annoyed him by knocking him with her pestle as she pounded yams. He then moved towards the heavens. The old woman tried to reach him by piling mortars up, but the pile collapsed, killing them all.

Floods and storms

The story of a great flood overwhelming the world is a popular myth. The earliest flood story comes from the Mesopotamian Epic of Gilgamesh, in which Utnapishtim frees birds to see if the waters are subsiding. The Native American Mandan tribe told of Lone Man, who survived a huge flood in his Big Canoe.

Saved by a fish

One day the Hindu wise man Manu found a fish in his washing water. The fish told Manu a flood was coming. The fish, an incarnation of Hindu god Vishnu, towed Manu to safety. Manu became the father of all humankind.

Giant Wave, a print of a tsunami (a huge, violent wave) by Katsushika Hokusai (1760–1849)

A tsunami is usually caused by a volcano or an earthquake; here, a tsunami batters a Japanese plank boat.

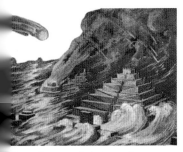

Kingdom of Atlantis

Poseidon, Greek god of the sea, loved a woman called Cleito. He built her an island where their sons founded the kingdom of Atlantis. Later rulers were greedy, so Poseidon sent a tidal wave to swallow Atlantis and its people.

Headdress of tropical bird feathers

Type of poncho (blanket-like cloak) worn by the Sapa Incas – rulers of the Inca empire

In his left hand, Chac carries a bowl; in his right is a ball of smoking incense.

Mayan rainmaker

Mayan rain god Chac broke open a rock to uncover the first maize plant. He sent rain to help the maize grow. Sometimes he sent storms and used his weapon of lightning.

Giant waves

The great flood is caused either by a deluge of rain, as in the Noah story, or by a tidal wave, as in the story of Atlantis. Both are images of unstoppable destruction.

Creator of humans

Viracocha, the Inca creator god, was unhappy with his stone humans, so he drowned them in a flood. He then made people from clay. The first Sapa Inca (Inca emperor) named himself after Viracocha.

Noah and the ark

When God saw how wicked humans had become, he decided to drown them all. But he chose to save one good man, Noah. He warned Noah to build an ark in which to save his family and two of every living creature, in order to repopulate Earth after the flood.

Some believe that gods live at the snowcapped peak of Mount Fuji in Japan.

Pele, Hawaiian goddess of fire

The elements

All over the world, the forces that shape our planet have been the focus of myth-making. Fire, air, earth, and water are known as the four elements in Western tradition. The Chinese have five elements: wood, fire, earth, metal, and water. Almost all mythologies tell how humans acquired the gift of fire, often stolen from the Sun. Gods of the air and the sky lead to the names of many supreme gods, such as that of Greek god Zeus, which means "sky".

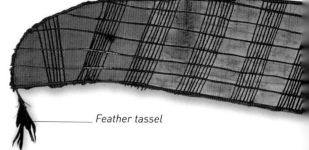

Feather tassel

Agni's stomach is full because fire devours everything.

Fire-eater
Wherever a fire is lit, the Hindu fire god Agni is born. He helped a man find his wife, who was taken by wise man Bhrigu. Bhrigu cursed Agni, making him consume Earth's dirt, but Agni purified it with his flames.

Volcanic Pele
In Hawaii, which is dominated by the Kilauea volcano, Pele is worshipped as the goddess of fire. She is as passionate and dangerous as a volcano.

Olokun, sea king of the Edo people of Benin, Nigeria

Oceans of Olokun
Olokun is the sea king of the Edo people of Benin, Nigeria. He is the bringer of children, whose souls must cross the ocean to be born. The Olokun River is the source of all Earth's waters, including the ocean.

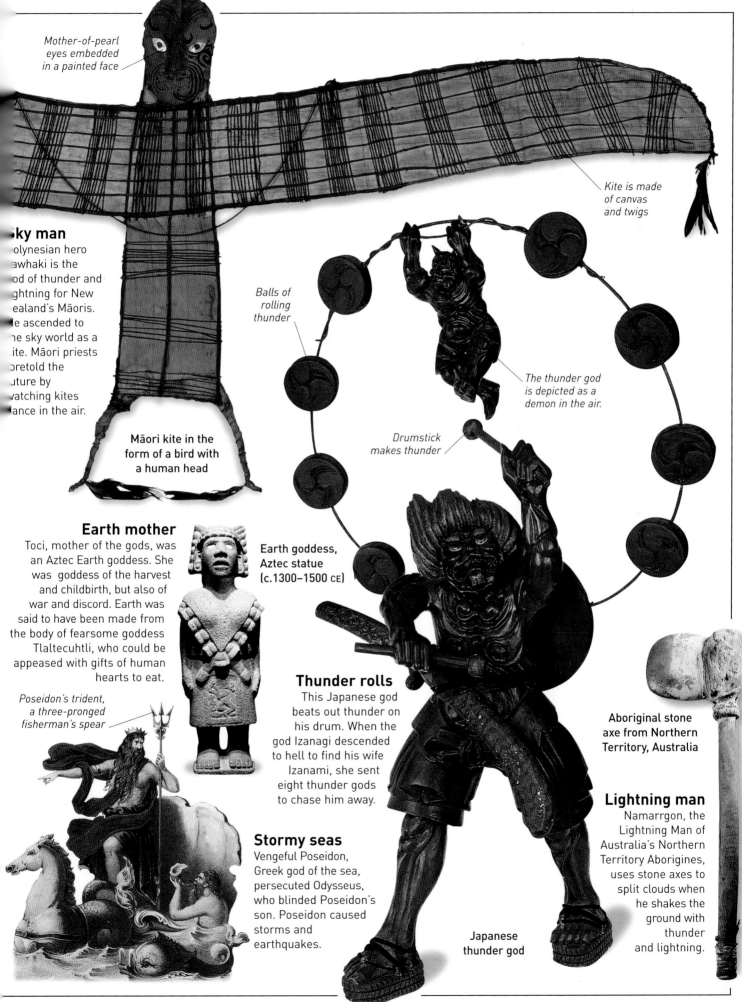

Mother-of-pearl eyes embedded in a painted face

Sky man

Polynesian hero Tawhaki is the god of thunder and lightning for New Zealand's Māoris. He ascended to the sky world as a kite. Māori priests foretold the future by watching kites dance in the air.

Māori kite in the form of a bird with a human head

Kite is made of canvas and twigs

Balls of rolling thunder

The thunder god is depicted as a demon in the air.

Drumstick makes thunder

Earth mother

Toci, mother of the gods, was an Aztec Earth goddess. She was goddess of the harvest and childbirth, but also of war and discord. Earth was said to have been made from the body of fearsome goddess Tlaltecuhtli, who could be appeased with gifts of human hearts to eat.

Earth goddess, Aztec statue (c.1300–1500 CE)

Poseidon's trident, a three-pronged fisherman's spear

Thunder rolls

This Japanese god beats out thunder on his drum. When the god Izanagi descended to hell to find his wife Izanami, she sent eight thunder gods to chase him away.

Stormy seas

Vengeful Poseidon, Greek god of the sea, persecuted Odysseus, who blinded Poseidon's son. Poseidon caused storms and earthquakes.

Japanese thunder god

Aboriginal stone axe from Northern Territory, Australia

Lightning man

Namarrgon, the Lightning Man of Australia's Northern Territory Aborigines, uses stone axes to split clouds when he shakes the ground with thunder and lightning.

The natural world

All the elements of the natural world are considered gifts of the gods. Many cultures worshipped Earth as a mother goddess, a provider of food and fertility. Specific gods took responsibility for crops. Hunting societies believe that game is withheld or released by the gods. In the forests of Cameroon, hunters pray to the ancestral spirits to release game from their divine stables.

This type of reed has been used to make pipes for 5,000 years.

Spanis reed

Cobs of maize

Pan's pipes
With goat-like horns and legs, Pan was the Greek god of the pastures, especially sheep and goats. Pan was very amorous. One nymph, Syrinx, turned into reeds to escape him. But Pan made musical pipes from the reeds so she would stay close.

Springtime god
Aztec god of spring Xipe Totec allowed his skin to be flayed (peeled off) to promote new growth from within – like a maize seed breaking through its husk to become a new plant.

Farmers harvesting rice

Rice supplies
Every village in Japan has a shrine dedicated to the rice god Inari, who comes down from his mountain home in the spring and returns in the autumn, after the rice harvest.

Rice grains

Wooden mask representing
the nature spirits of the
North American Inuits

Kelp
seaweed

Mother of sea beasts

Sedna, the Inuit sea woman, was
thrown into the sea by her father
because she married a dog. When
she tried to cling to the kayak,
he chopped off her fingers, which
became the first sea mammals.
Humans combed seaweed from
her hair, so Sedna released the
sea beasts to give humankind food.

*Mask represents the various
sea beasts, such as seals and
fish, that Sedna watches over*

Tane of the trees

Oceanic forest god Tane lived in the
highest heaven where he brought
three baskets of knowledge for
humankind. He made himself
a wife, Hine-hau-one (Earth-
formed maiden), from red sand.
This Māori ceremonial adze
(axe-like tool) symbolizes
Tane, who was himself
shaped by craftsmen
with adzes.

*Flora
awakens the
flowers with
sweet music
from her harp.*

Flowering flora

Flora was the Roman goddess
of spring who made plants and
trees bloom. She also had
a flower that made women
pregnant if they touched it.

Celtic bronze horse from a prince's tomb (c.5th century BCE)

Equestrian Epona
Epona, the Celtic horse goddess, is linked to the triple mother goddesses. She was also associated with horse breeding. The Celts farmed with horses, and they could not grow much food without them.

Fertility and birth

Worship of the great mother goddess, often identified as Earth, has been part of many cultures since the dawn of humanity. Pacha Mama, the Inca fertility goddess, means "Earth mother". When the Hittite god of farming, Telepinu, withdrew from the world and humans began to starve, it was mother goddess Hannahanna who found him. Birth and fertility were not just for goddesses. Frey was the Norse god of fertility, a role given in Egypt to the gods Min and Osiris.

Frey and Freya
Frey and his twin sister Freya were Norse fertility gods. Frey's cult involved his image being carried around in a wagon during winter to ensure fertility. Freya was primarily the goddess of love and soothsaying (predicting the future).

Goddess Freya in her chariot

Frey holds his beard, a symbol of growth, in one hand.

Jade skirt
Chalchiuhtlicue, She of the Jade Skirt, was the central Mexican goddess of lakes and, by association, the goddess of birth. She once flooded Earth, but turned humans into fish to save them.

Water goddess Chalchiuhtlicue stands in water with a giant centipede.

Native American Iroquois corn husk mask, worn in midwinter ceremonies to ensure a good harvest

Alabaster figurine of Ishtar c.300–200 BCE

Baby Horus

Love goddess
Ishtar, the Babylonian goddess of love, went to the underworld to rescue her husband Tammuz, god of plants. She died and the world withered. Ishtar returned to life, but for half the year Tammuz lives in the underworld as Ishtar laments. When he rises in spring, all rejoice.

Isis and Horus
The Egyptian goddess Isis is often shown nursing baby Horus, who was bitten by scorpions. Isis's anguished cries made Sun god Ra send for the god Thoth to cure the child.

First mother
Native Americans tell how First Father was born from sea foam and First Mother from leaf dew. The human race increased until there was famine. First Mother said, "My strength shall be felt all over Earth." She died and from her flesh grew the first corn.

Mould for making the casting of Venus (right)

Willendorf goddess
This stone figurine from Willendorf, Austria, shows a mother goddess and dates from the Neolithic period (c.5000 BCE).

Venus
Venus, the Roman goddess of love and fertility, was originally a goddess of farmland before being identified with Greek goddess Aphrodite, who was concerned with love.

Children of gods

In many myths, the gods reproduce as humans do. Their children may be other gods or semi-divine heroes, such as Cuchulain and Heracles. Some supreme deities, such as Norse god Odin and Greek god Zeus, are thought of as fathers, or heads of, their divine families. Not all offspring are good. Norse god Loki gave birth to the fierce wolf Fenrir, while Greek god Poseidon fathered the brutal Cyclops Polyphemus. Some Hindu gods incarnate in the form of children, like Krishna, an avatar of Vishnu.

Matsya, the fish

Kurma, the turtle

Incarnations of Vishnu
Hindu god Vishnu, the Preserver, has been incarnated nine times in different forms, called avatars. As a fish, Vishnu saved Manu, the first man, from the great flood. As a turtle, he churned the ocean. As a boar, he raised Earth from the sea. As the hero Rama, he rescued his wife from a demon.

Varaha, the boar

Cuchulain, in his human form, rides his chariot into battle.

Father of the Pharaohs
Falcon-headed Horus was the child of Egyptian gods Isis and Osiris. He was conceived when Isis breathed life into the mummified Osiris, who was murdered by his brother, Seth. Egyptian pharaohs, who traced their descent from him, were called the Living Horus.

Monstrous warrior
Cuchulain, a hero of Irish mythology, was a fierce warrior. His father was the Sun god Lugh. On the battlefield Cuchulain became a monster. One eye disappeared into his head, his heels turned to the front, and his jaws opened wide to swallow an enemy's head.

Prince Rama

The water twins
The Dogon people of Mali in Africa say the creator spirit Amma first mated with Earth, and the Nommo (water) twins were born. Human on the top and fish-like on the bottom, the twins (left) were made from the life force of Amma.

The Nommo stand between Earth and the sky on this Dogon leader's stool.

Heroic Heracles
The Greek hero Heracles (Hercules in Latin) was the son of Zeus by a mortal woman, Alcmene. As an infant he proved his divine nature by strangling two deadly serpents

Scary monsters

Giants are found throughout mythology. Their size makes them terrifying, but they are often portrayed as slow and stupid. Cyclops Polyphemus believed that the hero Odysseus's name was Nobody. When Odysseus blinded him by stabbing a poker into his single eye, he shouted, "Nobody is hurting me!"

Cyclopes had only one eye.

Incisors tear meat from bone

One-eyed ogre
Polyphemus was one of the one-eyed giants known as Cyclopes. The skulls of mastodons (extinct elephant-like mammals) were once thought to be those of Cyclopes.

Mastodon skull

Cyclopes had ferocious appetites and could devour carcasses in one sitting.

Cyclopes tore their prey limb from limb.

Tunic made from the hides of the Cyclops's prey

Ancestor worship

In many cultures, fear of the evil power of spirits of the dead is balanced by a belief in the protective power of the spirits of ancestors, who guide the living. Offerings are made to ancestor shrines. In China and Japan, wooden tablets inscribed with ancestors' names are kept in household shrines. In ancient Egypt, the eldest son of deceased parents had to raise a monument to their memory and say their names when he passed it, to keep their names alive.

Female figure, Middle Sepik River, Papua New Guinea

Romulus

Romulus, meaning "Roman", was the mythical founder of Rome. Twins Romulus and Remus were the sons of war god Mars. Abandoned as babies, they were suckled by a wolf. They argued over who should found Rome, and Romulus killed Remus.

Bronze Yoruba figurine from Benin, west Africa

Procession of Oshun devotees

Oshun worship

Ancestors are worshipped in Africa, and are prayed to for health, fertility, and fortune. The Yoruba people of west Africa worship Oshun, goddess of the river that bears the same name. People bathe in the Oshun River to protect against disease. Women consult Oshun about problems or illness.

Life-giving ancestors

In New Guinea, carved figures of ancestors were present at *moguru* (life-giving ceremonies), at which the young were initiated into adulthood. In the Papuan Gulf, fierce Kerua headhunters hung human skulls from carved boards as offerings to ancestors.

Colossal chiefs

On Rapa Nui (Easter Island), a remote and barren island of volcanic rock stranded in the eastern Pacific Ocean, stand hundreds of monolithic stone figures. They are *moai* – figures of dead chiefs who were regarded as descendants of the gods.

Feast of lanterns

The Bon festival, held annually in Japan, is known as the Feast of Lanterns. It is held in honour of the spirits of the dead, which return to Earth for the three days of the festival. Relatives of the deceased pray at shrines, where they leave food and treats for the spirits.

Dreaming ancestors

The Dreamtime is the eternal present in which the revered ancestors of the Australian Aborigines exist, constantly creating the world. Creation story designs, shown to the Aborigines by ancestors, are still painted on rocks and bark, like this painting from Arnhem Land.

Aboriginal stone knife, like those used by the eternal ancestors to create humans

Bark sheath

Papuan ancestral tablet, or ceremonial board

Gap-toothed Louhi as an eagle-woman

Bad Louhi

Finnish hag Louhi fought with the blacksmith Ilmarinen for the Sampo – a magic mill that grinds corn, salt, and money. When Ilmarinen stole the Sampo and set sail, Louhi turned into a bird and attacked the boat. The Sampo fell in the sea, where it still grinds out salt.

Evil forces

Besides gods of death, there are many demons and evil forces in mythology. Balanced against these are good forces. In a Siberian story, the creator Ulgan made himself a companion, Erlik, from mud floating on the primal ocean. Erlik betrayed Ulgan, and was sent to the underworld to sit alongside evil spirits. Evil beings are also active in Hindu myths, with many anti-gods and demons. The Mayan Vucub-Caquix was a monster macaw killed by hero twins Hunahpu and Xbalanque.

Treacherous trickster

Loki, the Norse trickster god, turned against the gods and brought about the death of Balder the Beautiful, son of the god Odin. For this, he is bound in agony, with poison dripping onto his face.

Vajrapani holds a thunderbolt in his right hand.

Tibetan statue of Vajrapani, the wielder of the thunderbolt, in his ferocious form

Fiery headdress encrusted with turquoise

Dark destroyer

The Tibetan Vajrapani destroys the wicked with his *vajra* (thunderbolt). He is one of eight Buddhist saints.

Baba Yaga uses her massive pestle (grinding stick) to stir up storms and spread disease.

Cannibal witch

Baba Yaga is the cannibal witch of Russian myth. She lives in a revolving hut supported by hens' feet, and flies in a big mortar (grinding pot).

Sulky Susano

The Japanese god Izanagi gave birth to three divinities: the Sun goddess Amaterasu, Moon god Tsuki-Yomi, and Susano, god of storms and chaos. Susano was meant to rule the sea, but he said he would prefer the underworld. Banished to Earth, he rescued Kusa-nada-hime, the rice paddy princess, from an eight-headed dragon, and made her his wife.

Text from a 19th-century print of the storm god Susano and his wife

Kusa-nada-hime, the Japanese rice paddy princess

First human sacrifice

When Aztec goddess Coatlicue was pregnant with the supreme god Huitzilopochtli, she was killed by her daughter Coyolxauhqui. Huitzilopochtli leapt fully formed from his mother's body, and slew his sister, making her the first human sacrifice.

Each of Durga's 10 hands holds a special weapon – a symbol of divine power.

Invincible Durga

Hindu warrior goddess Durga was one of the guises of the great goddess Devi. Durga was created to fight the *asuras* (demon enemies of the gods), who had conquered heaven.

Susano, the Japanese storm god

Superheroes

Men and women who achieve great feats of daring and courage are celebrated in all mythologies. Often, they are said to be the children of gods, or to be specially favoured by the gods. Some heroes can defeat a whole series of enemies in single combat and rid countries of the monsters that plague them. Others are celebrated as peacemakers rather than as warriors.

Polynices's corpse is left to rot.

Antigone

Antigone was the daughter of Oedipus, King of Thebes, Greece. When he died, his sons, Eteocles and Polynices, fought over the throne and killed each other. Their uncle Creon buried Eteocles with honour, but left Polynices to rot. Antigone defied Creon and gave Polynices a burial. Creon put her in a cave, so she hanged herself.

When Krishna plays his magic flute, women within earshot join him to dance.

Krishna is always blue to show he is an incarnation of Vishnu.

Krishna stands on a lotus flower, symbol of Earth

Wampum (bead) belts were made to mark peace agreements.

Beads are made from white and purple clam shells

Demon dodger

Krishna is the eighth avatar (incarnation) of Hindu god Vishnu, and is worshipped as a god in his own right. As a child, his mother took him to the countryside to escape demon king Kansa, who was persecuting them. Kansa sent a female demon to poison him, but Krishna sucked the life out of her.

Peacemaker

Dekanah-wida was born to bring peace from the Chief of the Sky Spirits to warring Native American tribes. He made Mohawk chief, Hiawatha, peacemaker. They formed the Iroquois League and the members swore peace.

Sigurd kills the dragon.

Dragon slayer

Scandinavian hero Sigurd slew the dragon Fafnir to claim its treasure. Sigurd was told to kill the dragon by Regin, Fafnir's brother, who asked for the dragon's heart. But Regin wanted to kill Sigurd and steal the treasure. Birds warned Sigurd but he did not understand. As Sigurd cooked the dragon's heart, he got burned and tasted dragon blood. Sigurd finally understood the birds' message, killed Regin, and kept the treasure.

Fafnir the dragon

When Yi shot the Suns, they fell to Earth in the shape of crows.

Theseus

The Minotaur had a bull's head on a man's body.

Monster killer

Athenian hero Theseus slayed the Minotaur, which was part man, part bull. King Minos of Crete fed the Minotaur with Athenian children. Theseus killed the Minotaur in its labyrinth (maze).

Yi won a potion of immortality, but his wife Chang E drank it and floated to the Moon.

Yi

The Chinese believe in 10 original Suns – all sons of the Emperor of the Eastern Heavens. They took turns to light the sky, until all 10 went out and scorched Earth. The Emperor sent Yi, the heavenly archer, to teach them a lesson. He shot down nine of them.

Heavenly gates are guarded by two soldiers

Mortals on their way to heaven to become immortals

Perseus holds Medusa's severed head.

Greek guardian

Perseus was the son of Greek god Zeus and the maiden Danaë. Perseus agreed to get the head of the gorgon Medusa, whose glance turned people to stone. Using a shield as a mirror to avoid the gorgon's gaze, Perseus cut off her head.

Kneeling men and women mourn for the dead.

Altars full of food

Gilgamesh clutches a captured lion cub.

Scenes of the underworld

The body of Medusa

King Gilgamesh

A hero of ancient Mesopotamia, Gilgamesh was a semi-divine king who fought monsters. When Gilgamesh scorned the love of goddess Ishtar, she sent a bull to destroy him, but Gilgamesh slew it.

Chinese funeral banner, 2nd century BCE

Journeys and quests

Setting out on a journey to complete a set task, or going in search of something special, is a common theme in myths. The adventures of people who are sidetracked on their way home, like Odysseus's action-filled return from the Trojan War, are also popular tales. In many cultures, both creation and death are explained as mythological journeys.

Jason and the Golden Fleece

In a Greek myth, Jason was a young man who was sent out on a quest to find the Golden Fleece. He built a fine ship, the *Argo*, and set out with his brave men, the Argonauts. After fighting giants and other creatures, they found the ram's fleece, overcame the ferocious dragon that guarded it, and returned home successfully.

Sirens – mysterious, bird-like women with alluring voices

Osiris judges who can join the Afterlife.

Odysseus, tied to the mast to prevent him from jumping into the sea

A dead person respectfully enters the Hall of Osiris.

Odysseus

On his way home from the Trojan War, the Greek hero Odysseus met many monsters and obstacles. When he came across the sirens, whose beautiful voices lured sailors to their deaths, he tied himself to the mast of his ship to listen in safety, while his men plugged their ears and rowed on.

Journey through the realm of Osiris

The ancient Egyptians prepared carefully for the journey that would lead them to the Afterlife. They were buried with the *Book of the Dead*, which listed handy spells and advice for the underworld voyage towards Osiris, king of the dead.

Rainbow Snake

In Aboriginal creation mythology, known as Dreamtime, the Rainbow Snake came out of a water hole. He travelled the country, creating the hills, valleys, and rivers of Australia as he slithered across the ground. Then, he arched above the land, in the form of a rainbow.

Princess Damayanti chooses a husband.

Together at last

Hindu princess Damayanti marries King Nala for love, but by choosing him, she angers the gods. They are sent into the woods but get separated. The princess returns home, but Nala is turned into a dwarf and goes off to serve another king. To get her true love back, Damayanti pretends to look for a new husband. Nala turns up, as a dwarf, but she realizes it is him and they are happily reunited.

A bark painting of Rainbow Snake creating the land

Hill

Sinbad fights a sea monster that has captured his friend Hakeem.

Sinbad the Sailor

One of the tales in *One Thousand and One Nights*, a medieval Arabic collection of stories, tells of Sinbad the Sailor, a young man from Baghdad who sails off to seek his fortune. He is shipwrecked, but his luck turns and he returns home rich. Adventure tempts again, and he sets off on another six journeys, each full of exciting events and each seeing him return richer than before.

Angels appear as Sir Galahad nears the grail.

Sir Galahad kneels in awe before the Grail.

The Grail, shown as an ornate cup, is guarded by angels.

The Holy Grail

Many of King Arthur's knights went out in search of the legendary Holy Grail. For the knights, the quest was a way to show their honour, virtue, and courage. It wasn't enough to locate the Grail; once it was found, only the purest of heart could lay eyes on it. Finally, it was Sir Galahad who brought this epic quest to an end.

This depiction, by Sir Edward Burne-Jones (1833–98), shows Sir Galahad finding the Grail

Divine weapons

Sword, spear, axe, or bow, the weapons of the gods often mirror those of humans. The Norse all-father Odin had a magical spear to stir up war. The gods can unleash natural forces as weapons, such as the thunderbolt (lightning) – a weapon of sky gods. Weapons could be improvised, with semi-divine Greek hero Heracles using an olive tree as a club. Gods can punish the wicked without weapons. When Greek hunter Actaeon spied goddess Artemis without her bow and arrows, she turned him into a stag, so his hounds mauled him to death.

Greek god Zeus wields a thunderbolt.

Bad blood
This 19th-century chief's axe is a symbol of Tane, Oceanic god of the forests, who was shaped by craftsmen with axes. After Tane separated Earth and sky, he and his brother Tangaroa, god of the seas, began a battle. Tangaroa lashed the land with his waves. Tane supplied men with canoes, spears, and nets to catch Tangaroa's fish.

Shango looks both ways so no one can escape him.

Thunder and lightning
Electrical storms are considered by many to be the anger of the gods. Thunderbolts have been used as weapons by many gods, such as Zeus of ancient Greece. Many Native Americans revere the Thunderbird, which makes thunder by flapping its wings, and lightning by flashing its eyes. Tupan, an Amazonian thunder god, caused storms by crossing the sky in a dugout canoe.

Spitter of thunderbolts
Ceremonial staffs like this symbolize Shango, thunder god of the Yoruba people of Africa. His symbol is the double axe, which represents thunderbolts. Shango was originally a king, and was given the power to spit thunderbolts by trickster god Eshus.

To terrify Shango's enemies, his devotees hold thunderbolt staffs as they dance to loud drumbeats.

Magical sword
Norse god Frey had a sword that would fight on its own. It is said that at the final battle of Ragnarok, Frey will fight the fire giant Surt, who has a blade that flames like the Sun. But without his sword, Frey will be defeated, allowing Surt to burn up the world.

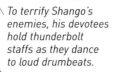

Iron sword from Denmark

Ancestral weapon

The boomerang was an important weapon for Australian Aborigines. The first boomerang represented the Aboriginal Rainbow Snake and is said to have been made from the tree between heaven and Earth.

Rainbow Snake

Aboriginal war boomerangs are designed to fly in straight lines and travel great distances.

7th-century brass *vajras* from Tibet, representing thunderbolts

Tibetans use vajras, believed to hold magical powers, in rituals and while meditating.

Blade of iron

Ogun is the god of iron and war among the Yoruba people of west Africa. When Earth was still a watery waste, Ogun climbed down from heaven on a spider's web to hunt in the marshland. After Earth formed, Ogun cleared the land with his iron blade. He was last seen sinking into the ground with his sword.

Ritual sword used in Ogun worship

Vows taken in the name of Ogun, with the tongue on a blade or some other iron object, are binding.

Ceremonial bow and arrows

Goddess of hunting

Diana is the Roman name for Artemis, the Greek goddess of hunting and archery. Although Diana was the goddess of the hunt, she was also the protector of wild animals.

Diana, Roman protector of wild animals

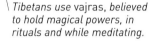

Silver replica of Thor's hammer from Denmark

Thor's lucky hammer

Norse thunder god Thor was the son of the all-father Odin; his mother was Earth. He had a hammer, Mjollnir, which never missed its target, and always returned to his hand. Vikings wore pendants in the shape of Thor's lucky hammer for protection.

Thor in his chariot pulled by goats

Gods of war

Human history has been shaped by war and conflict, and gods of war have a high status in many mythologies. Ancient Greeks had two war gods: Ares, the god of fighting, and Athena, the goddess of strategy. Most war gods are male, and many, like Ares and Odin, are bloodthirsty, revelling in slaughter. But in Mesopotamia, Ishtar was goddess of love and war.

The divine blacksmith Gu taught the first humans how to make tools so that they could work the land.

Mars wears a warrior's helmet.

Greek goddess of strategy
Athena was goddess of strategy and wisdom. She sprang from the head of her father Zeus, fully armed and ready for battle. Athena is always depicted in armour, with the head of the gorgon Medusa fixed to her breastplate.

Protective Mars
Mars was the Roman god of war. He was originally a god of agriculture, and even as a war god, he retained a protective function. He was an important Roman god who was believed to have fathered Romulus, the founder of Rome.

God of iron
Gu was the fifth child of Mawu-Lisa, the west African creator god who passed on her strength. He is made of iron, and is sometimes depicted as an iron sword. In this form, Mawu-Lisa used him to clear Earth for humans to live on. Gu is the god of iron and also war, as war is waged with iron weapons.

Warring Ku
War god Ku of Hawaii had many names. As patron of woodworkers, he was Ku-Adzing-Out-the-Canoe. When the gods were trapped between their parents, Earth and Sky, Ku-of-the-Angry-Face wanted to kill them, but the gods fought Ku. This was the beginning of warfare.

Iron statue of Gu, war god of the Fon people of west Africa

Fighting spirits

The valkyries of the Viking (Norse) god Odin were female spirits who rode to battle to give victory or death, according to Odin's will. They also waited on the souls of dead warriors in the hall of Valhalla (heaven). The name valkyrie means "chooser of the slain".

Valkyries rode horses to fetch dead warriors from the battlefield and take them to Odin's Valhalla.

Norse all-father Odin sacrificed one of his eyes in return for wisdom.

Chinese bronze sword, 4th century BCE

Norse war gods

The Viking (Norse) gods were among the most warlike of all. Their leader, Odin, was the god of battle, inspiring his berserker warriors with a fighting frenzy.

Spears were among a Viking warrior's most prized possessions.

Demon killer

Skanda, the Hindu god of war, is the son of Shiva. He was born to kill the demon Taraka. Skanda rides a peacock around the world in a learning contest with his brother Ganesha, who stayed at home, reading. When Skanda returned, Ganesha knew more.

Chinese warrior god

Guan Di is the Chinese god of war. Once a seller of tofu (soybean curd), he devoted himself to study. But he killed a magistrate, fled his home, and became a soldier, one of the three Brothers of the Peach Orchard. In 1594 CE, he was given god of war status.

Statue of Guan Di, the Chinese god of war

Contacting the spirits

Ancient Greeks took their problems to the oracle of Apollo at Delphi, where a priestess called the Pythia (Pythoness) went into a trance and uttered words for a priest to interpret. Among the Vikings, volvas (prophetesses) answered questions in a similar way. Siberian shamans, Native American medicine men, and Australian Aboriginal karadji, all use drumming, dance, and song to enter an altered mental state in which they can communicate with the spirit world.

Guiding god
Greek god Hermes (Mercury in Rome) was the messenger of the gods, and also the guide of souls into the underworld.

Pipe of carved human bone

Priest speaks into this hole to distort his voice and make it boom out

Voice disguiser
A priest of the Tiv people of Nigeria used this voice disguiser to allow the ancestor god Tiv to speak through him in a piercing cry.

Half-halo represents Ganesha's divinity

Noose to trap delusion

Jizo, the protector of children and travellers

Conveyor of prayers
Ganesha, the wise elephant-headed son of Shiva, is god of good enterprises. Hindus ask Ganesha to pass on requests to Shiva and make him offerings before planning journeys or weddings.

豊川閣靈驗守護攸

Good-luck charms
Japanese *fuda*, or amulets, bear a god's name. They are used to ward off evil and bring good luck. They are placed on household shrines to protect the family.

The ancestors sit in the top of the world tree; the shaman climbs up to ask for their help.

Shaman's spirit helpers can take animal forms

Drumbeats are used to call the spirits that will help the shaman.

Metal ornaments hanging from the belt protect against evil spirits.

The shaman

Shamans are believed to have had a life-changing vision that enables them to enter a trance and fly to the spirit world. A shaman's power is usually used to heal, although it may also cause disease or death.

Souls of the unborn nest in the tree.

Dancers hung from rawhide thongs sewn through the skin

Sun Dance

In customs like the Sun Dance, Plains Native Americans performed painful rituals as sacrifices to the Great Spirit. Dancers hoped to receive a vision afterwards.

The pipe bowl is round, like the world, and outside is the Universe.

Pipes of peace

The sacred pipe is a key part of many Native American rituals, bringing peace and healing. Tobacco was believed to summon good spirits and ward off evil ones.

The world tree houses all souls.

Spirit

Tiger spirits often teach shamans their craft.

Siberian shaman's outfit

Love and fortune

Many people worship deities who will bring them luck in life. The Ewe people of Togo in west Africa believe that the soul of each unborn child must visit Ngolimeno, the Mother of the Spirit People, who will grant them a happy life. The Japanese worship Seven Gods of Luck, of whom one, Benten, is a goddess. The Chinese worship many gods of fortune and happiness. The lucky Ho-Ho twins are often shown attending Tsai Shen, the god of wealth.

Winged god
Cupid (Eros in Greek) was the Roman god of love, often shown as an infant with a bow and arrows. His gold-tipped arrows made people fall in love.

Detail from Botticelli's painting The Birth of Venus (c.1486)

Born of foam
The Greek goddess of love and desire, Aphrodite, known as Venus to the Romans, was born from sea foam. She devoted herself to pleasure, never did any work, and was often assisted by Eros (Cupid to the Romans).

Each twin carries a jar containing a lotus of purity and perfection.

Terracotta figure of Aphrodite, 2nd century BCE

Born from sea foam, Aphrodite floated ashore on a scallop shell.

The gods are standing on beds of lotus flowers.

The head of each twin is decorated with a lotus.

Good fortune gods

The Japanese Seven Gods of Luck (Shichi Fukujin) are Bishamon, Daikoku, Ebisu, Fukurokuju, Hotei, Jorojin, and the goddess Benten – bringer of love, happiness, and fortune. The Shichi Fukujin are often shown on their treasure ship. Their treasures include a hat of invisibility, a lucky rain hat, and a purse that never empties.

Benten rides an ox, a symbol of good fortune

Confused deity

Kwan-non is the god or goddess of mercy in Japanese Buddhism. Priests regard Kwan-non as a male divinity, but most people pray to him as a goddess, and he appears in 33 female forms. This statue shows her (or him) with a baby.

The Ho-Ho gods, symbolizing happy couples

Love medicines are placed in the pockets of each doll.

Love dolls

These Native American medicine dolls are used by the Menominee of the western Great Lakes to ensure that a husband and wife stay faithful. The male doll is named after the husband and the female doll, after the wife, and the two are tied together face to face.

Ho-Ho twins

The two immortals called Ho are the patrons of Chinese merchants. Besides bringing prosperity, they represent harmonious union between couples, because the word *ho* means harmony.

Tricksters

Light comedy and dark humour are introduced into myths by trickster figures, such as the Native American Coyote, whose mischief leads to havoc. Tricksters may be animal, human, or both. Some tricksters hover between good and evil, like the Norse god Loki. The Ashanti people of west Africa tell tales of Anansi, the cunning spider-man who won all the world's stories from the sky god Nyame. Since then, these tales have been called spider stories.

Wily coyote
Many Native American peoples tell stories of the wily Coyote, who both tricks and is tricked. Coyote is greedy and selfish, and his exploits lead to bad or good consequences.

Cowrie shells are used by Eshu to predict the future.

Mischievous Eshu
Eshu is the trickster god of the Yoruba people of west Africa. He loves mischief, and his many guises include giant, dwarf, cheeky boy, wise old man, and priest, as seen here.

Eshu holds a small statue of himself.

Mask worn to impersonate Hare

Hare climbs up the mask

Cunning hare
Hare is an African animal trickster known in America as Brer Rabbit. Cunning and wily, Hare outwits the other animals, except when Tortoise challenged him to a race. Instead of running, Tortoise put his family members around the course and waited for Hare at the finish line.

Eshu in his various guises

An Eshu priest wore this statue by hooking the headdress over his shoulder, as Eshu is doing with the statue.

Sun catcher

Maui-Of-A-Thousand-Tricks is the trickster hero of Polynesian mythology. He fished up the islands with his magical hook, pushed up the heavens, and stole fire for humankind.

The tengu rescue the hero Tametomo from the jaws of a giant fish.

Medicine calabashes represent Eshu's magical powers.

Invisible tricksters

The tengu are Japanese trickster spirits, part bird, part man. They are said to come from storm god Susano, who himself got into trouble by playing tricks. The tengu have magic cloaks of invisibility.

Grimacing god

Bes was a popular god of music, dance, and laughter in ancient Egypt. His grimace and antics were thought to scare off evil spirits. He was protector of mothers in childbirth. He is always shown sticking his tongue out at the world.

Bacchus's long, flowing hair shows his eternal youth.

Fish represents the islands that Maui fished from the sea

Indulgent god

Bacchus (Dionysus in Greek) was the Roman god of wine and ecstasy. His followers were wild women called the Maenads (Frenzied Ones). Bacchus gave King Midas the double-edged gift of turning all that he touched into gold.

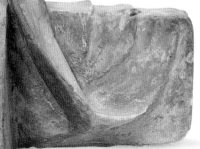

Giants and small folk

Many stories tell of creatures of unusual dimensions. Size doesn't always reflect power, or character – little beings can be just as powerful, or mean, as big ones (and often smarter, too). In Hindu mythology, gods can change their size at will, especially when punishing those who have offended them.

Tiny god of love

Venus, the Roman goddess of love, has a son called Cupid. This mischievous little boy will aim his arrow at unsuspecting victims, who are gripped by love when hit. In ancient art, Cupid is shown as a teenager, but in later representations, he becomes younger and smaller, before taking on the now familiar shape of the chubby, winged baby boy.

Sculpture of a troll living under a bridge, like the one in the tale of The Three Billy Goats Gruff

This peculiar-looking boulder could be home to Huldufolk.

Terrifying troll

Most trolls are huge, dwelling in mountains or dense forests. Sometimes, they will steal food, treasure, or even babies from humans. Anybody lured away by a troll should take care not to eat troll food as humans who taste it will never return home again.

Death of a demon

The god Vishnu as a gigantic man-lion

In Hindu myth, the demon king Hiranyakashipu is protected by a blessing that says that he can't be killed by animal or by man, by any weapon, by day or by night. When Hiranyakashipu wants to murder his own son for praying to Vishnu, the god gets angry. He appears at twilight, as a huge half-man, half-lion, and uses his nails instead of a weapon. The blessing is of no use and Hiranyakashipu dies.

Hiranyakashipu

Part of nature

Iceland's magical landscape is home to the Huldufolk, or "hidden people". These little elves and nature spirits make their home in rocks and boulders. If disturbed by humans, they can cause chaos.

Tumbling down the beanstalk

In *Jack and the Beanstalk*, the young boy, Jack, outwits the dangerous but slow-witted giant who lives in a castle at the top of the magic talk. When Jack escapes down the beanstalk the giant chases after him, but Jack chops it down and the giant falls to his death.

The farm caretaker

On farms throughout Scandinavia, the Nisse, a small, crumpled, old man with a grey beard, is traditionally a highly appreciated, but rarely seen, presence. He looks after the animals and the farm, and also its people, as long as he is well treated by the humans – giving him sweet porridge at Christmas is essential.

The giant takes a tumble when the beanstalk is cut down.

Jack clutches the axe while his mother looks on.

Rübezahl's staff helps him stride across the mountains.

Lord of the mountain

In German and Czech tales, the giant Rübezahl is a stern-looking man, also known as the Lord of the Mountain. He protects travellers in the mountains, as long as they are respectful of him, and of animals and nature. If not, he will use his powers to cause avalanches, bad weather, or simply confuse them and make them lose their way.

Kraken's tentacles hold the ship's masts in a vice-like grip.

Giant of the seas

A Scandinavian myth tells of Kraken, a huge sea monster that destroys ships. It would appear suddenly from the depths and throw its powerful tentacles around the ship. Once it dived again, ship and crew would be dragged down to a certain death.

Animal idols

Gods and spirits may be shown in animal form or as half-human, half-beast. Trickster figures, such as African spider-man Anansi, may be a man, an animal, or a mix. Other gods transform into animals. Greek god Zeus became a bull and then a swan. Gods can have animal doubles. Aztec god Quetzalcoatl had a twin called Xolotl, a dog who brought the bones of humankind back from the underworld.

The bull of heave
This winged bull stoo
guard over a royal palac
in Assyria. The bull wa
a cult animal all ove
ancient west Asi

Drinking horns tipped with sheep's heads

The horned one
Gods with animals' horns are found in many myths. The Celtic horned god Cernunnos was lord of the beasts and a fertility god.

Nagas, sacred snakes, have both protective and destructive powers.

Half-human, half-beast

Nearly all the ancient Egyptian gods have at least one animal form. The cow goddess Hathor was also worshipped as the lioness Sekhmet and the cat Bastet. The dog or jackal god Anubis could also become a snake or a falcon. Sun god Ra turned into a cat to cut off the head of the evil snake Apep.

19th-century Sri Lankan mask

The snake demon
This mask of Naga Rassa, or Snake Demon, is worn in dances to drive away evil spirits. The nagas (sacred snakes) were descended from the ancient sage Kasyapa, the father of life.

Fierce face wards off evil spirits thought to cause sickness

Sekhmet
The Sun god Ra sent the lioness Sekhmet to destroy humankind. But when Ra changed his mind, the only way to stop Sekhmet killing was to make her drunk.

Sobek
Egyptian crocodile god Sobek, son of the creator goddess Neith, was lord of the River Nile. He was shown as a crocodile or a man with a crocodile head.

Anubis
The jackal-headed god Anubis made the first mummy when he wrapped the body parts of the god Osiris in cloth to put them back together.

When Garuda soars into the sky, he symbolizes the human spirit.

Golden Garuda's body shines as bright as the Sun – some say he was the Sun in a bird form.

Vishnu and his wife, Lakshmi, rode on Garuda

Garuda has the body of a human.

Clawed foot enabled Garuda to pick up the snakes that he devoured

Eagle-like wings

Leg covered with golden feathers

King of the birds

Half-human, half-bird, Garuda was the Hindu king of the birds. He was ridden by the god Vishnu. Garuda was the son of Kasyapa. He hated his father's other offspring, the nagas, because their mother made his mother, Vinata, an underworld slave. To save her, Garuda stole a cup of the elixir of immortality.

Brass figure of Garuda from Tibet

Mythical beasts

Native Americans say that many monsters existed until heroes defeated them. Some people think mythical beasts are based on garbled accounts of real creatures, for example, unicorns are really rhinoceroses. Monsters can be a mix of animals, like the griffin, which was half-eagle, half-lion. Giving an ordinary animal a special feature makes it extraordinary, like the flying Greek horse Pegasus.

Wild horses
Half-man, half-horse, the centaur was a savage creatur One exception was Chiron, a wise centaur who tutored many Greek heroes.

Sea monsters
In the past, sailors returned from their travels with strange beasts, which they claimed to have fished from the sea. This creature, known as Jenny Haniver, is a dried skate fish.

Spiky claws protrude from the dragon's wings.

Blowing hot air
Fire-breathing winged dragons who guard their treasure feature in many European myths. Norse (Viking) dragon Fafnir was a man who turned into a dragon to protect his treasure. Many stories tell of dragon-slaying heroes who rescue maidens. Unlike the fearsome European dragons, Chinese dragons are kind and serpent-like.

Dragons breathe fire.

Horn of purity

The unicorn was a white, horse-like creature with a single spiral horn. It was said that if a unicorn dipped its horn into water, the water would become pure. Supposed unicorn horns (actually the tusks of narwhal whales) once sold for 20 times their weight in gold.

Unicorn horns were prized for their ability to clear poison from water.

Dreadful locks

The gorgons were three snake-haired sisters, Stheno, Euryale, and Medusa. Stheno and Euryale were immortal, but Medusa was mortal, and was slain by Greek hero Perseus.

Ship's emblem depicting the gorgon Medusa

Wings of a hero

The winged horse Pegasus was ridden by the Greek hero Bellerophon. When enemies ordered Bellerophon to kill the monstrous Chimera, they hoped he would die. Instead, riding Pegasus, Bellerophon swooped down on Chimera and riddled it with arrows.

Greek coin showing the winged Pegasus

A serpent formed the Chimera's tail.

The middle part of the Chimera was a she-goat.

European dragons have bat-like wings.

Thorny hooks protrude from the dragon's tail.

Heads and tails

The Chimera was a fire-breathing monster made up of various animals. It was one of the children of the half-nymph, half-serpent Echidna, who also spawned such monsters as the Sphinx and the 100-headed serpent, Ladon.

The Chimera had the forequarters of a lioness.

The dragon's skin is covered with scales, like those of a serpent or fish.

Clawed feet are seen on both Chinese and European dragons.

Shapeshifters

Creatures that can change form appear in myths worldwide. Some are divine messengers, while some change into men or women to share temporarily the human world. Others are cursed beings who cannot co-exist peacefully with humans, and some use shapeshifting to gain power and wealth.

Selkie or seal?
In Scottish and Irish folklore, Selkies are sea-dwelling creatures that can turn from being seal-like to human and back again. They shift by shedding their magical seal skins, but they mustn't lose these when in human form, or they can never return to the sea again.

Enchanted dolphin
According to legend, some dolphins in the Amazon River are the Encantado (enchanted one) and can shapeshift into young men, who come ashore at night. They have magical powers and humans should avoid looking into their eyes.

Clever as a fox
Japan's Kitsune are very special foxes. As they age, gaining power and wisdom, they also acquire more tails, and can have up to nine. They can take on human form, often as women, and are also divine messengers of Inari, the Shinto patron of foxes, rice, and prosperity.

The Monkey King wears a crown topped with two phoenix feathers.

The Monkey King in his monkey shape, one of his 72 different forms

Kelpies

Kelpies are Gaelic water spirits, believed to live in Scottish rivers, streams, and small lochs. They usually appear in the shape of a horse, and might seem friendly enough to ride. But people, and children in particular, should stay away, because as soon as a Kelpie has got anyone on its back, it will dive back into the water, drowning its rider. Sometimes, they take on human form, but a careful look will reveal that they still have hooves instead of human feet.

Monkey magic

In Buddhist mythology, the Monkey King begins life as a stone egg, which takes the shape of a monkey and then comes alive. He becomes king of the monkeys and gains various supernatural powers. He can change into no less than 72 transformations, which helps him achieve what he wants.

This film still of a werewolf shows some clearly human features among the fur.

Werewolf

People have always feared wolves, but the werewolf is even more terrifying. Once transformed by the full moon, it cannot stop itself attacking anyone. Wolf-men appear in ancient myths, but traditional werewolf tales really took off in the late Middle Ages, and reputed attacks were still reported in the 18th century.

Some vampires, like the famous Count Dracula, can turn into bats.

Vampire at night

Eastern European legends of vampires became a top theme of the "Gothic" horror novels of the 19th century. The classic vampire is a pale nobleman, doomed to live forever and always on the hunt for human blood, turning his victims into vampires by biting them. Only a wooden stake struck through the heart will kill them.

Painting the story

Many myths are told through ritual, dance, or art rather than through narrative storytelling. In the chantways of the Native American Navajo, sand-painting, song, prayer, dance, and ritual combine to recreate complex myths, which are remembered for their healing spiritual power. Australian Aboriginal stories of the Dreamtime are traditional designs used in bark paintings, ground paintings, and body paintings.

Beating the drum
Across Africa, drums beat out rhythms to accompany rituals and dances. Drums are thought to have spirits inside. This *bata* drum was used by the Yoruba tribe of Africa to honour thunder god Shango.

The headdress varies in size and design, according to the character.

Noble characters paint their faces green.

Heroes wear red jackets.

Ankle bracelets

The skirt is made up of many layers of white cotton.

Stories through dance
Kathakali dancers enact stories from the two great epics of India, the *Mahabharata* and the *Ramayana*. The essence of both is the eternal struggle between good and evil.

Beats of the double-sided drum call up new creations.

Wooden snake stick

Snake dance
Native Americans hold rituals to ensure good crops. In the Hopi Snake Dance, dancers hold snakes in their mouths. After the dance, the snakes are released to take the prayers to the gods.

Ring of flames
Hindu god Shiva dances the Tandava, which represents the creation and destruction of the world. He dances in a circle of flames.

Sacred sand-paintings

The sand-paintings of the Native American Navajo are temporary altars created and destroyed as part of healing rituals known as chantways. Their Navajo name means "place where the gods come and go".

Mudstone

Sandstone

Gypsum

Chalk

Brown pigment

Yellow pigment

Red pigment

Charcoal

Only men can become qualified sand-painters.

Pigments are trickled onto sand through the thumb and forefinger

The Oculate Being has bulging eyes.

Powder paints
Sand-painting pigments are gathered by the family who sponsor the ceremony, and ground in a mortar and pestle. Pigments include sandstone, mudstone, and chalk.

Chantway ceremonies
Sand-paintings are made by skilled painters led by the singer, who oversees the ritual. As the painting is finished, the singer sprinkles it with pollen, says a prayer, and the ritual begins.

Powerful pictures
Sacred sand-paintings contain depictions of the Navajo Holy People – supernatural beings whose powers are evoked in the chantway ceremonies. This non-sacred sand-painting, made for commercial sale, shows a typical Holy Person.

Bracelets and armlets hang from the wrists and elbows.

Snake-like tongue

Woven story
This woven textile from the Paracas people of Peru is full of the spirits and demons of Paracas mythology, including bug-eyed Oculate Beings, shown as heads with long tongues.

Alpaca wool weaving from southern Peru, 600–200 BCE

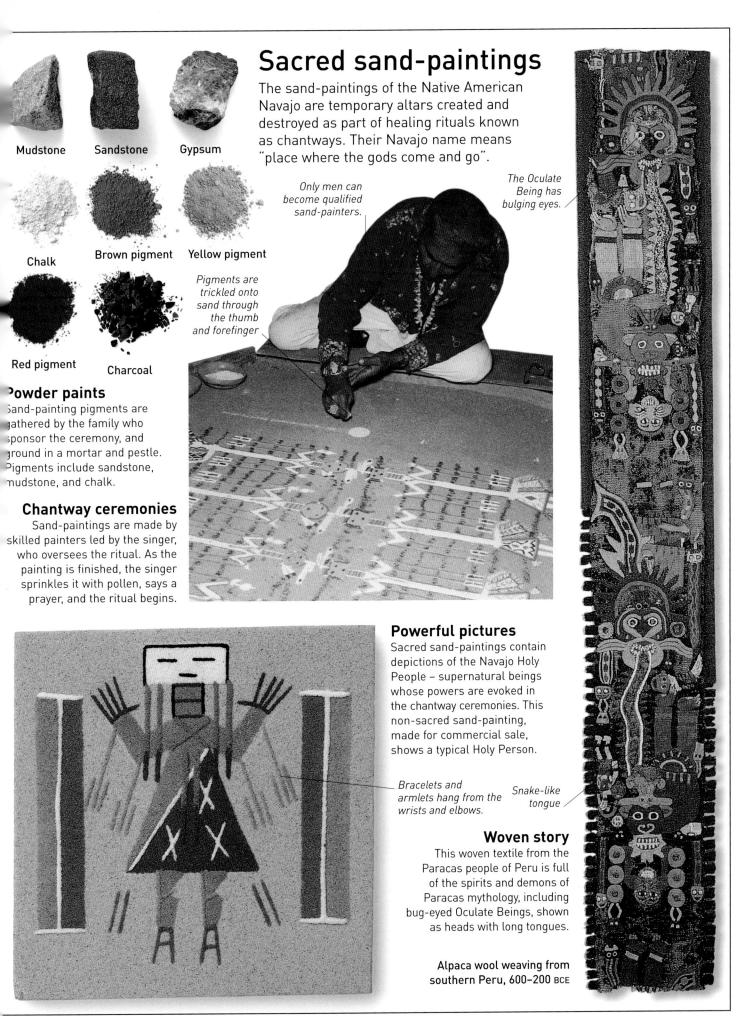

Universal creatures

Turtle tale
Many Native American peoples believe that Earth is supported on the back of a turtle – a belief that is also found in Hindu mythology. In one myth, the creator god Brahma took the shape of a turtle to create the world.

Many common themes run through mythology. One theme connects humans with other animals. We are either descended from them, they are our reincarnated ancestors, or they represent gods o spirits to be worshipped. In many creation myths, such as the Australian Aboriginal stories of the Dreamtime, the first inhabitants of the world are a mix of animal and human. This is true of anima gods, such as the African spider-man Anansi.

Eyes of inlaid turquoise

Native American Anasazi frog, a symbol of water

Frog
A west African story of how Frog brought death is echoed by a Native American myth telling how Frog was so angry with his Maker that he spat poison into the water, killing his Maker. To the Māoris of New Zealand, the frog was a rain god.

Crocodiles
Crocodiles appear in many myths as threatening creatures. The Basuto tribe of Africa believes a crocodile can seize a man's shadow and pull him under water. On the island of Sulawesi, in Indonesia, crocodiles are called Grandfather because they may be an ancestor. It is believed that a crocodile will attack a human only when told to do so by the god Poe Mpalaburu.

Detail from a Papuan shield

Man inside the belly of a crocodile

Coral pieces add colour to the nose and mouth

Ceremonial snake pendant worn by priests of the Aztec rain god Tlaloc

Turquoise mosaic squares

Life-giving serpent
The snake is the most widely revered creature in world mythology. It is associated with the primal waters from which all life was created. In the Americas, the double-headed serpent is associated with life-giving rain. Many Australian Aborigines credit the creation of the landscape to the Rainbow Snake, the source of magical power.

Crocodile-men
In Papua New Guinea people believe crocodiles have magical powers. One myth tells how the creator Ipila carved the first four humans from wood, and gave them sago to eat. But two of them began to eat meat, and turned into crocodile-men.

Egyptian crocodile god Sobek

The crocodile has large snapping jaws with very sharp teeth.

Mayan crocodile incense burner

Clawed feet

Golden crocodile figure made by the Ashanti people of west Africa

Heavenly monster
In Mayan art there are many depictions of the celestial, or cosmic, monster – a being with a crocodile's body and two heads. The monster is shown arching over the heavens, its body in the form of clouds.

Dry, scaly skin prevents water loss in the hot African climate.

Nile crocodile

Back feet are webbed

Powerful, whip-like tail

Nile crocodiles are found on riverbanks throughout tropical Africa.

African ancestors
Many Africans believe crocodiles are reincarnated people. In west Africa, it is said that a person who kills a crocodile will become one. If someone is attacked by a crocodile, it is thought the victim must have harmed the crocodile during its human life.

Ravenous Sobek
Ancient Egyptians worshipped crocodiles in the form of the crocodile god Sobek, who had a crocodile's head and a human body. Sobek was so hungry that, when the body of Osiris was thrown in the River Nile, he ate some of it. The other gods cut out Sobek's tongue for this wicked act.

The afterlife

People have always told stories about what happens after death. Mayan hero twins Hunahpu and Xbalanque went to Xibalba to rescue their father from One Death, the underworld lord. They survived and let themselves be killed to show their power over death. When they came back to life, the impressed death lords asked to be killed, too. But the twins did not revive them, and the power of death was lessened forever.

The skeleton is commonly used as an image of death

Chinese judge of the dead
Yen-lo is the terrifying ruler and judge of the dead in China. The souls are weighed before they must pass a number of tests and challenges. Finally, each soul is reincarnated

Dying for disobedience
The funeral rites of the Dogon people of west Africa involve dancing and chanting in a secret language. These rituals recount a myth that death entered the world because of disobedient young men.

Osiris, Egyptian god of the underworld

Horus, son of Osiris

Weighing of the souls
Ancient Egyptians believed their souls would be weighed against the feather of truth. They would then face Osiris, lord of the dead. They hoped for a new life in the Field of Reeds, a perfect version of Egypt.

Skirts are red to represent death

Aztec lord of the underworld

Mictlantecuhtli, Aztec god of death, is depicted as a skeleton spotted with blood. On their way to his peaceful underworld (Mictlan), the dead were reduced to skeletons by a wind of knives.

Day of the Dead

On the Mexican Day of the Dead (1 November), families in Mexico pray to the souls of dead relatives to return to Earth for a night. Altars are decorated with food, flowers, and ghoulish sugar models. A candle is lit to help each soul find its way back.

Altar skulls are made from sugar and water, and are decorated with icing sugar.

Demons torment the souls of the dead.

Depiction of the Christian hell

Mictlantecuhtli welcomes the dead to his underworld.

Visions of hell

Eternal torment in an underworld, such as the Christian hell, is the fate of sinners in many cultures. The Greeks devised ingenious fates for those upsetting the gods. Sisyphus, who told tales on Zeus, spent eternity rolling a stone uphill, only to see it roll back down as he reached the top.

Viking chieftains were cremated in longboats to take them to Valhalla.

Warrior heaven

Viking (Norse) warriors longed to be chosen for death in battle by Odin's warrior maidens, the valkyries. Instead of hell, warriors enjoyed a glorious afterlife of feasting and fighting in the golden halls of Valhalla (heaven).

White pottery figure of the Aztec lord of death

Sacred sites

The ice-age cave pictures of Europe – and their ancient equivalents in Australia, America, and Africa – show us that humankind has always recognized sacred spaces, where the everyday and the eternal meet. Sacred sites may be temporary or permanent, and the same place may be re-used many times. Many Christian churches, for example, are on the sites of pagan temples. Lakes, rivers, caves, woods, or mountain tops can be just as spiritual as a temple or church.

Great pyramids
The Egyptian Sun god Ra was born on a pyramid-shaped piece of land jutting out of the primal ocean. This shape was adopted by the pharaohs (kings) for their tombs.

Most probably an altar, this flat sandstone block was 5 m (16 ft) in length.

Standing stones
The Neolithic temple at Stonehenge in Wiltshire, UK, was built between 2500 and 1500 BCE. The sacred stones are aligned with the Sun, Moon, and stars.

Curved ends reach up to heaven

Entrance to heaven
A *torii* is a gateless entrance marking the point where ordinary space becomes sacred space. A *torii* stands at the entrance to each Japanese Shinto shrine, and also the sacred Mount Fuji.

The thunderbird makes lightning by opening and closing its eyes.

The Thunderbird creates thunder by flapping its wings.

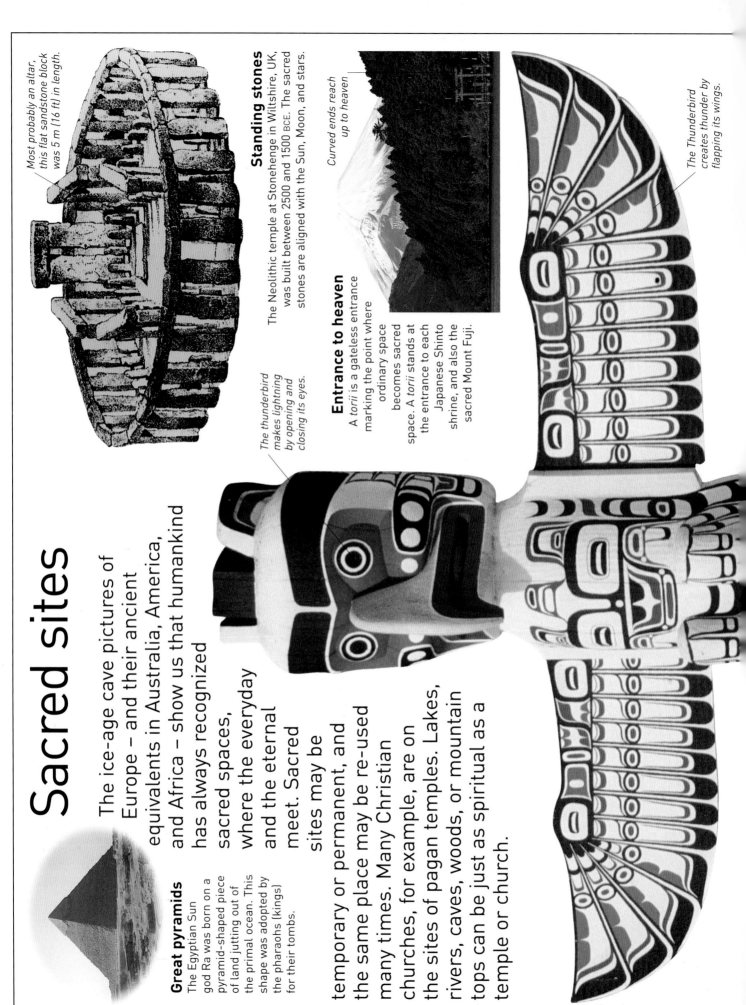

Mythical monuments

The totem poles of Native Americans are carved heraldic monuments displaying images of a family's mythological descent. The Native American Kwakiutl people say that the first totem pole, Kakaluyuwish (Pole That Holds Up The Sky), was made by Wakiash, a Kwakiutl chief, with knowledge he gained from the animal-people when Raven flew him around the world.

Thunderbird totem pole in Stanley Park, Vancouver, Canada (1988 copy of an original that was erected in 1927)

Temple of the maiden

The ancient Greek word *parthenon* means "temple of the maiden", and the Parthenon was the great temple of Athena on the Acropolis at Athens, Greece. Athena, the goddess of war and wisdom, was patron of the city.

Golden waters

Gold was so important to the Peruvian Incas that they called it the sweat of the Sun god Inti. At El Dorado lake in Colombia, each new king was coated in gold dust before sailing out to throw gold offerings into the water.

Majestic mountain

The sacred site of Uluru, or Ayers Rock, rises from the central desert of Australia with natural majesty. The Aborigines of central Australia said Uluru was built in the Dreamtime by two boys playing with mud.

At sunrise and sunset, Uluru displays spectacular shades of orange and purple.

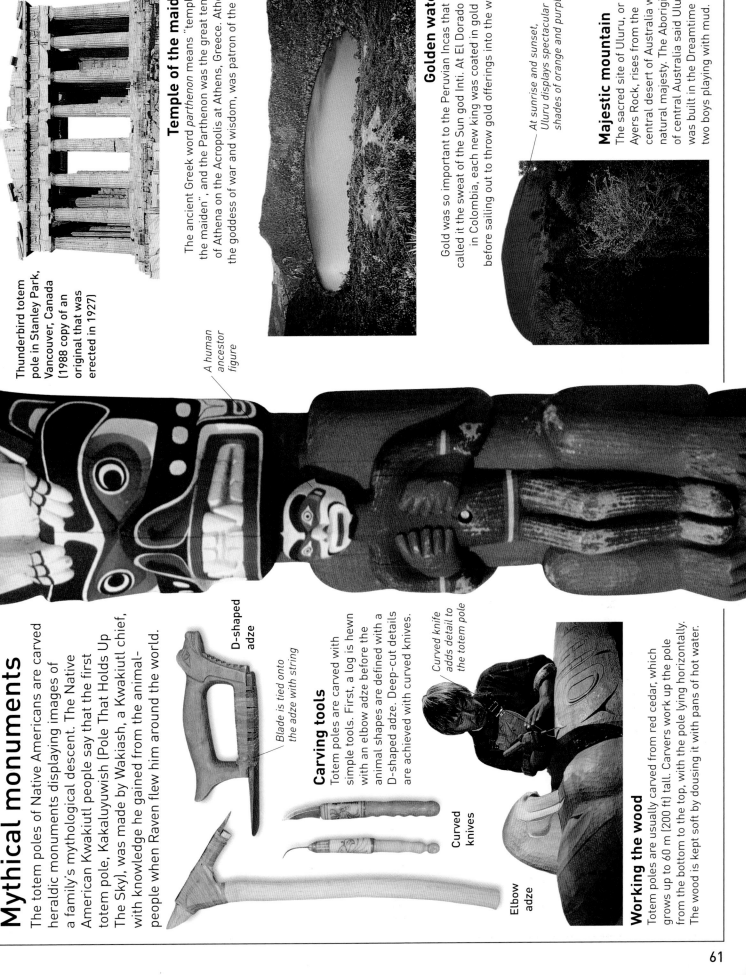

A human ancestor figure

Blade is tied onto the adze with string

D-shaped adze

Carving tools

Totem poles are carved with simple tools. First, a log is hewn with an elbow adze before the animal shapes are defined with a D-shaped adze. Deep-cut details are achieved with curved knives.

Curved knives

Elbow adze

Curved knife adds detail to the totem pole

Working the wood

Totem poles are usually carved from red cedar, which grows up to 60 m (200 ft) tall. Carvers work up the pole from the bottom to the top, with the pole lying horizontally. The wood is kept soft by dousing it with pans of hot water.

End of the world

The world will end when the rainbow serpent chews his own tail.

Cosmic serpent

In west Africa, Aido-Hwedo, the Rainbow Snake, carried the creator in his mouth as the world was made, and circled around the Earth to hold it together. Monkeys beneath the sea forge iron bars to feed him. When the iron runs out, Aido-Hwedo will chew his own tail and Earth will slide into the sea.

Just as mythologies tell how the world began, so they predict how it will end, often in a fire or flood. Aborigines of southeastern Australia believed the end would come when a prop that held up the sky rotted away, allowing the sky to fall. To the Native American Cherokee, the world was a great floating island, held by four cords hanging from the sky, and when these rotted, Earth would sink back beneath the sea.

Rocky matter from an explosion in space

The world serpent has many heads.

When Brahma awakes, he rises on a lotus flower from the god Vishnu.

Lakshmi, Vishnu's wife, goddess of fortune

At night, Vishnu rests on the world serpent, Shesha.

End of the *kalpa*

For Hindus, time is an endless cycle of days and nights of Brahma, or *kalpas*. In the day, when Brahma is awake, the world is created anew. When Brahma goes to sleep, the *kalpa* ends. Each *kalpa* lasts 4,320 million years.

Great world pole

According to the Native American Cheyenne people, the Great White Grandfather Beaver of the North is gnawing the pole that holds up the world. When he gnaws right through it, the world will end.

North American family totem (symbol) of the beaver

Aztec calendar stone (c.1352)

Myth of the five suns

According to Aztec belief, this is the fifth world, and each creation has its own Sun. The fifth Sun first shone on 13 August 3114 BCE, and will last until at least 4772 CE. It will not last forever, for "all moons, all years, all days, all winds, reach their completion and pass away."

Sun god Ra in the guise of a cat

Apep, the chaos serpent

Egyptian Apep

As the Sun god Ra sailed through the underworld, his ship was attacked by chaos serpent Apep, his mortal enemy. If Apep devoured Ra, the world would end. Ra took the form of a cat and cut off Apep's head.

Thor fights the Midgard serpent.

Big Crunch

Many myths envisage a cycle of creation and destruction, and foresee a new world when this one ends. Scientific theory believes this is feasible. The Universe, which is expanding, may reach a maximum size and collapse in on itself in a Big Crunch. Matter and energy may bounce back to create a new Universe.

Last battle of the Norse gods

The warlike Vikings (Norsemen) thought the world would end in a final battle, in which Earth would be consumed by fire. This battle is Ragnarok, the "Twilight of the Gods". But from this world's ruin, a new creation will arise.

Did you know?

Myth and Fact

Mexican Tree of Life

The Sphinx was a mythical monster sent to punish the people of Thebes in Greece. She gobbled up anyone who did not solve her riddle: "What walks on four legs, two legs, and then three?" The answer was "man". He crawls on all fours as a baby, then walks on two legs, and has a third leg in old age – a walking stick!

The Canaanites of the Middle East had a grisly way of placating thunder god Baal. In a new house, a couple sacrificed a child and buried it under the foundations.

Archaeologists have unearthed evidence to explain the trances of the Pythia – the priestess at Delphi, ancient Greece. Ethylene gas was escaping from faults in the rock, and this would have made the Pythia hallucinate. In her trance, she believed the god Apollo spoke to her.

A butterfly, symbol of the Pima creator god

The Pima Native Americans believed Great Butterfly, the creator god, flew down and made the first people from his own sweat. Across the Pacific, a tribe on the island of Sumatra, Indonesia, thought its ancestors had hatched from butterfly eggs.

One west African myth tells how the Earth mother, Iyadola, made the first people from clay. Some were white, because they were not fired enough. Some were fired too long and burned black. Others came out yellow, brown, or pink.

Some modern Mexican artists create images of the Tree of Life. They incorporate gods and other figures from Mayan and Aztec mythologies, mixed up with symbols borrowed from the Catholic Church.

On the Indonesian island of Java, *wayang kulit* (shadow puppet) plays enact myths. The puppeteer operates the puppets. The audience sees the shadows on a screen.

Javanese *wayang kulit*, made from leather

According to an old Indian legend, the coastal town of Mahabalipuram in southern India had seven temples until the gods sent a flood to destroy the town. Today, one temple stands on the seashore, but in 2002, divers found evidence of six more temples under the sea.

The Giant's Causeway on the Antrim coast, Northern Ireland, is named after giant Finn MacCool. He built a causeway of huge stepping stones across the sea to Scotland. In reality, volcanic activity formed the basalt stones about 60 million years ago.

In 2001, an archaeologist found the earliest picture of the Mayan corn god, from 100 CE. The corn god went to the underworld but was resurrected.

One Greek myth tells how Leto turned mean peasants into frogs. The peasants did not want her to drink from their lake, so they muddied the water with sticks. To punish them, Leto decided they would stay croaking in the mud forever.

Part of the Giant's Causeway in Antrim, Northern Ireland

There are many versions of how Arthur became king of the Britons. In one, Arthur proved his right to kingship by drawing Excalibur, an enchanted sword, from a stone.

In Norse (Scandinavian) mythology, a serpent was thought to lie coiled around the world on the sea bed. Norwegian sailors later believed in the *kraken*, a many-armed sea monster that was 2.4 km (1.5 miles) across and capable of pulling a ship down into the ocean.

Questions and Answers

Tupan Patera crater on Jupiter's moon Io, as seen from the *Galileo* spacecraft

Q Do any of the planets have mythical associations?

A All of the planets in our Solar System, apart from Earth, are named after gods or goddesses. These are taken from the Roman pantheon (family of gods), with one exception – Uranus was the primordial sky god in Greek myth. The remaining six planets are named after Mercury, speedy messenger of the gods; Venus, goddess of love; Mars, god of farming and war; Jupiter, king of the gods; Saturn, god of the heavens; and Neptune, god of water.

Q Do any other places in our Solar System have mythical names?

A Many moons are named after characters from myths. Martian moons Phobos and Deimos take their names from two sons of Ares, the Greek god of war. Astronomers recently discovered a volcanic crater on Io, and that, too, has a mythical name – Tupan Patera, named after the Brazilian thunder god. It is about 75 km (47 miles) across and extremely active.

Temple of Kukulkan in Mexico

Q How does a Sami shaman drum up the spirit world?

A The Sami people live in northern Europe, across Finland, Norway, Sweden, and Russia. In some areas, they still live as they have done for centuries. Traditionally, each tribe has a shaman called a *noaide* who looks after the people's spiritual health. He casts spells and tells prophecies. The shaman summons up the spirit world by entering a trance. He performs rituals such as beating a magical drum called a *runebom*.

Q Which pyramid spoke in the voice of a god?

A Many experts agree that the Mayan Temple of Kukulkan at Chichen Itza, Mexico, produces echoes that sound like the cry of a quetzal bird, but not all are convinced that the pyramid's acoustics were intentional. The quetzal was sacred to the Maya. It was linked to their god Kukulkan, the quetzal serpent – the same god as Quetzalcoatl, who was worshipped by the Aztecs. If a priest stood at the base of the temple steps and clapped, the pyramid answered in the divine quetzal's voice.

Q Which animal links the Kongo world with the next world?

A In traditional rituals, the Kongo people of Central Africa use carved objects called *nkisi* to call the spirits. *Nkisi* can be filled with magical herbs. One popular *nkisi* is Kozo, the dog. The Kongo believe dogs inhabitat both the land of the living and the land of the dead.

Kongo carving of Kozo (late 1800s)

Record Breakers

OLDEST MYTHICAL PAINTINGS
Cave art found at Chauvet-Pont-d'Arc, France, dates back 31,000 years. It probably depicts myths, and includes animal figures.

OLDEST WRITTEN STORY
Parts of the Babylonian *Epic of Gilgamesh* have been found on clay fragments dating from 1700 BCE, but the story originated from 3000 BCE.

OLDEST ANCIENT WONDER
The Great Pyramid at Giza, Egypt, is the oldest survivor of the seven wonders of the ancient world. It was built around 4,500 years ago.

Mythical meanings

Elements from the natural world can have symbolic meaning in myths. Here are the meanings attached to some plants.

Lotus flower

APPLE
The Norse (Scandinavian) gods ate the golden apples of Idun, goddess of spring, to stay young. There were golden apples in Greek mythology, too. The hero Heracles managed to steal them, but first he had to kill Ladon, the 100-headed dragon guarding them.

ASH
Yggdrasil, the World Tree of Norse mythology, was a mighty ash. The Vikings (Norsemen) believed the first people were carved from the wood of ash trees.

Cherries

CHERRY
The Chinese thought the cherry tree was a lucky symbol of spring. In Japan, samurai warriors used the cherry fruit as their emblem, perhaps because its blood-coloured flesh hid a tough, strong kernel.

DATE
In the deserts of north Africa and the Middle East, the date was a main source of food often linked with fertility. The ancient Egyptians associated the date palm with the Tree of Life, and pictures of date palms decorate their temples.

FIG
The Romans said their god of wine, Bacchus, created the fig. They also believed that their city's founders, Romulus and Remus, were suckled under a fig tree by the River Tiber.

IRIS
The iris was the namesake of the Greek rainbow goddess. In Japanese folklore, irises protected homes from evil.

IVY
The Greek god Dionysus was found under an ivy bush as a baby. He was often shown crowned with ivy and carrying an ivy-entwined staff. Ivy came to stand for longevity.

JUJUBE TREE
The Taoists hold that the fruit of the jujube tree was food of the gods. The tree's spiny branches were sometimes believed to have protective powers.

LAUREL
The laurel was linked to Greek god Apollo. Daphne, the nymph he loved, was turned into a laurel to escape him, so he wore a laurel crown ever after. Victorious Roman generals wore laurel wreaths.

LILY
The lily was associated with the Greek goddess Hera – it was said to have sprung from her milk. It was also a symbol of purity or prosperity.

LOTUS
Lotus flowers made up the crown of Osiris, the ancient Egyptian god of the underworld. The flower was an emblem of rebirth, because it rose from the River Nile. The lotus is also key to the Hindu and Buddhist faiths as a symbol of Earth and creation.

Roots made to look like humans

Medieval print of a mandrake

Ancient Egyptian painting showing a date palm

MANDRAKE
The mandrake was thought to have magical powers because of its roots, which often resembled human figures. The plant was said to scream when uprooted – and the sound was enough to kill a person! In Greek myth, the sorceress Circe used mandrake root in her spells.

Trailing ivy

MARIGOLD

The Chinese link this orange flower with the Sun and longevity. In India, it is the sacred flower of Krishna.

Watercolour painting of a myrtle branch

MYRTLE

With its evergreen leaves and sweet scent, myrtle was linked with the Greek goddess of love, Aphrodite. It came to be a symbol of marital love and childbirth. In China, the plant was associated with success.

NARCISSUS

In Greek mythology, Narcissus was a beautiful youth who fell in love with his own reflection in a pool. Unable to move from the pool, he wasted away. This flower is often a symbol of early death.

Narcissus flowers

OAK

The oak represented might and longevity across Europe. In Greek mythology, Heracles's club was made of oak wood, as was Jason's ship, the *Argo*. According to the Romans, the sky god Jupiter was sheltered under an oak as an infant. The Druids often held their sacred rites under oak trees.

OLIVE

Olives were a source of oil and food for ancient civilizations in the Mediterranean. In Greek legend, goddess Athena made the olive bear fruit. In Japan, the olive is a symbol of friendship and success.

PLUM

In China, the plum tree is associated with happy marriages and longevity, partly because it blooms so early.

POMEGRANATE

The pomegranate is a symbol of fertility. When Persephone was in the underworld with Hades, she ate a pomegranate seed – this condemned her to spend four months of every year in the underworld.

Poppy

POPPY

Traditionally, the poppy was an emblem of sleep, death, and the soothing of pain because of opium properties found in poppies.

ROSE

In Roman myth, the red rose sprang from the blood of the love goddess, Venus. She had caught her foot on the thorn of a white rose while running to be with her dying lover, Adonis.

ROSEMARY

The herb rosemary is known to have healing powers, but in European folklore, it was used to protect against witches, fairies, evil spirits, and even storms. The Romans connected it to the goddess Venus.

Athena, ancient Greek goddess

TAMARISK

The tamarisk is a desert-growing tree that produces edible resin. In ancient Egypt, it was connected with the god Osiris. The Chinese held the tamarisk to be a symbol of immortality, and the Japanese associated it with rain.

VINE

The grapevine is the source of wine, and it was linked with Greek god Dionysus and Roman god Bacchus. Followers of these gods drank wine to bring them closer to the divine. Bunches of grapes often symbolized fruitfulness and drunkenness.

WILLOW

The Ainu people of Japan said that a willow branch formed the spine of the first man. The Chinese connected willow with strength and flexibility.

YEW

The yew tree lives to a great age, so it appears as a symbol of immortality.

Find out more

Mythology is all around you, but you may not even notice it. Creatures of ancient myth pop up in modern stories and movies. You can find books or web pages that retell classical myths. In art galleries, the paintings depict gods and heroes. Some of your traditions and festivals may be rooted in ancient myths.

Amphitheatre on the Acropolis, Athens, Greece
Ancient Greek playwrights drew on their mythological heritage. Many of their works are performed today in theatres around the world. One of the most amazing venues is an ancient amphitheatre. The Odeon of Herodes Atticus was built around 161 CE.

Mythology at the movies
Movie-makers often look to myths to find plots for their films. In *Jason and the Argonauts*, made in 1963, the Greek hero Jason is on a quest for the Golden Fleece. He slays the dragon guarding the fleece and steers his ship through two moving cliffs.

The sea god Poseidon

Jason's ship was the Argo, *so his crew were called Argonauts.*

Standing stones at Carnac, France
Many ancient sacred sites can still be seen. At Carnac, in southern Brittany, France, there are more than 3,000 stone monuments. They have been standing there for 6,000 years – since the Stone Age.

Corn dolly
Perhaps you have seen or made a corn figure. Made with the last sheaf of the harvest, it contained the spirit of the corn.

Bacchus and Ariadne (1521–1523)
This painting by Titian is at the National Gallery in London, UK. It shows Bacchus, Roman god of wine, when he first saw the princess Ariadne. He turned her crown into stars, so Titian painted stars above Ariadne's head.

Halloween spooks
Halloween has its roots in Celtic rituals. The festival Samhain, on 1 November, honoured the Celtic Lord of the Dead.

USEFUL WEBSITES
- An online encyclopedia of mythology and folklore
  www.pantheon.org
- An archive of source texts on mythology and religion
  www.sacred-texts.com
- A guide to gods, heroes, and monsters of Greek myth
  www.mythweb.com
- Site about Egyptian gods at the British Museum
  www.ancientegypt.co.uk/gods

PLACES TO VISIT

BRITISH MUSEUM, LONDON, UK
- Largest collection of Egyptian artefacts outside Cairo
- Mesoamerican treasures
- A Rapa Nui (Easter Island) statue
- Online access to the collections at www.britishmuseum.org/explore/highlights.aspx

CAMBRIDGE UNIVERSITY MUSEUM OF ARCHAEOLOGY AND ANTHROPOLOGY, CAMBRIDGE, UK
- Around 750,000 objects in total
- More than 30,000 Pacific artefacts
- 20th-century collection of British folklore

MUSÉE DE L'HOMME, PARIS, FRANCE
- Giant Rapa Nui (Easter Island) statue
- Magical charms and amulets

MUSÉE DU LOUVRE, PARIS, FRANCE
- Paintings of gods and monsters, such as Correggio's *Venus, Satyr, and Cupid*
- Antiquities from ancient Egypt, including statues of Bastet and Sekhmet
- Greek and Roman statuary, including the *Venus de Milo* (c.100 BCE)

MYTHSTORIES MUSEUM, WEM, SHROPSHIRE, UK
- The only UK museum dedicated to myths from around the world
- Interactive exhibits
- Reference library

SMITHSONIAN INSTITUTION, WASHINGTON, DC, USA
- More than 140 million objects, artworks, and specimens
- Includes the National Museum of the American Indian and the National Museum of African Art

Cat goddess
If you want to come face to face with an ancient god, visit a museum. This statue of the Egyptian goddess Bastet is on display in the Louvre, Paris, France. Many large museums have collections to help you find out about ancient myths.

Glossary

ADZE
An axe-like cutting tool.

AFTERLIFE
A life after death.

AMULET
A magical charm worn to bring good luck or ward off evil.

ANCESTOR
Someone from whom a person is descended.

ARCHAEOLOGIST
Someone who studies ancient artefacts.

AVATAR
A Hindu god taking a physical form.

BIG BANG
The explosion that created the Universe 13 billion years ago.

BODHISATTVA
A Buddhist saint worthy of nirvana, who remains with humans to help them.

CENTAUR
A mythical creature, half-man and half-horse.

CHIMERA
A mythical fire-breathing monster with three heads – a lion's, a goat's, and a serpent's.

Model of the Chimera

Krishna, an avatar (incarnation) of Vishnu

COSMOLOGY
The study of order in the Universe.

COSMOS
The whole world or Universe, seen to be arranged in an order.

CULT
A group of believers devoted to a spiritual leader or divine figure.

CYCLOPS
In Greek mythology, a one-eyed giant (plural: Cyclopes).

DEITY
A god or goddess.

DEMON
A devil or evil spirit.

DIVINE
Describes a god.

DRAGON
A mythical fire-breathing monster with a huge scaly body, wings, and a tail.

DREAMTIME
The eternal present in which the sacred ancestors of the Australian Aborigines shaped the world. Aboriginal myths take place in the Dreamtime.

DRUID
A Celtic priest.

ELIXIR
A liquid possessing magical powers, such as granting immortality.

FERTILITY
The ability to produce children or grow crops.

GORGON
In Greek mythology, one of three serpent-haired sisters – Stheno, Euryale, and Medusa.

GRIFFIN
A mythical creature, half-eagle, half-lion.

IMMORTAL
Able to live forever.

INCARNATION
The appearance of a god in physical form.

INITIATED
Accepted or admitted into a group.

Painted lotus-shaped tiles from an ancient Egyptian temple

KALPA
In Hindu cosmology, a period in which the Universe experiences one cycle of creation (when Brahma is awake) and destruction (when Brahma sleeps).

KATHAKALI
A classical dance-drama from Kerala, southern India, usually performed by men and boys.

KAYAK
A sealskin canoe used by the Inuit.

Map of Mesoamerica

LAVA
Hot molten rock that erupts from a volcano or an opening in Earth's crust.

LOTUS
A water lily growing in Egypt or India.

MACE
A ceremonial staff or war club.

MESOAMERICA
An ancient region of Central America. Before the 16th-century Spanish conquest, Mesoamerica was home to civilizations like the Aztecs and Maya.

MILKY WAY
Our galaxy, a family of star systems held by gravity, including our Solar System.

MORTAL
A being that lives for a certain amount of time and then dies.

MUMMIFIED
A body turned into a mummy – preserved so it will not decay.

MYTH
A story about gods or heroes that often explains how the world came to be or how people should live in it. In everyday speech, the word "myth" can mean an untruth.

NEOLITHIC
From the New Stone Age, which began around the time of the last ice age. Neolithic people used complex stone tools, built stone structures, and made pottery.

NIRVANA
The state of supreme happiness and enlightenment in Buddhism and Hinduism.

NORSE
Scandinavian; from Sweden, Norway, or Denmark. Vikings were Norse people who flourished from the 8th to 11th centuries CE.

NYMPH
In Greek mythology, a beautiful young woman who had one divine parent.

ORACLE
A place where the words of a god are revealed, or the person through whom a god speaks.

PAGAN
A person who follows a religion other than Christianity, Judaism, or Islam.

PHARAOH
The title given to the kings of ancient Egypt.

PRIMORDIAL
Existing at or from the beginning of creation.

PYRAMID
A stone structure with a square base and sloping sides. Pyramids could be royal tombs, as in Egypt, or sacrificial temples, as in Mesoamerica.

REINCARNATION
The belief that a dead person is reborn in another body (as per MORTAL note above).

Aztec sacrificial knife

Ritual mask worn by an African shaman

RESURRECTION
Rising from the dead, or being restored to life.

RITE
A religious or spiritual ceremony.

RITUAL
A formalized set of words in which gods are worshipped or asked for help.

SACRED
Holy or revered.

SACRIFICE
An offering made to please a god, usually at a cost to the giver.

SHAMAN
A priest or medicine man who protects the spiritual welfare of a tribe by holding rituals to influence good or evil spirits.

SHRINE
A sacred place dedicated to a god, spirit, or holy object.

SOOTHSAYING
Telling fortunes or predicting the future.

SORCEROR
A wizard or magician who casts spells and has magical powers.

SPIRIT
A bodiless person or being.

SUPERNATURAL
Magical or spiritual.

TORII
The entrance to a Shinto temple, usually painted red.

TOTEM
A Native American name for a spiritual ancestor. A totem can be a living creature or an inanimate object.

TRIBE
A group of related people who share the same language and culture.

TRICKSTER
A person or god who plays tricks or deceives.

TSUNAMI
A huge sea wave, usually triggered by a volcano or earthquake.

UNDERWORLD
A mythical region below Earth where people are said to live after death.

VALHALLA
In Norse (Scandinavian) mythology, the great hall of Odin, where dead heroes feast and fight in the afterlife.

VALKYRIE
In Norse (Scandinavian) mythology, one of the female battle spirits who guide heroes to Valhalla.

VISION
A mystical or religious experience in which a person sees a god or spirit.

Viking stone from the Swedish island of Gotland, showing a Norse warrior riding into Valhalla on Odin's eight-legged horse

Index

AB

Aborigines 6, 7, 21, 29, 35, 37, 40, 54, 56, 61, 62
Adam and Eve 15
adze 23, 61
Africa 6, 10, 14, 16, 17, 20, 22, 26, 28, 36, 38, 40, 42, 44–45, 48, 54, 56, 57, 58, 62, 64, 65
Agni 20
Aido-Hwedo 14, 56, 62
Amaterasu 13, 31
Anansi 44, 48, 56
Antigone 32
Anubis 48
Apep 63
Aphrodite 25, 42, 67
Apollo 16, 40, 64, 66
Ares 38, 65
Ariadne 33, 69
Artemis 12, 16, 36, 37, 64
Arthur, King 64
Ashanti people 16, 17, 44, 57
Athena 38, 61, 67
Atlantis 19
avatars 26, 32
Aztecs 16, 21, 22, 31, 48, 56, 59, 63, 66
Baal 16, 64
Baba Yaga 30
Babel, Tower of 7
Babylon 7, 11, 13, 16, 20, 25, 65
Bacchus 45, 66, 67, 69
Bastet 48, 69
Bes 26, 45
Bible 7, 15, 19
Brahma 6, 10, 14, 56, 62
Buddhism 30, 43, 48, 66

CD

Celts 7, 24, 48, 50, 60, 69
centaur 50
Cernunnos 7, 48
Chac 19
Chalchiuhtlicue 24
chantways 54, 55
Chimera 51
China 6, 10, 14, 17, 20, 28, 33, 39, 42–43, 50, 58, 59, 66, 67
Christianity 56, 59, 60
Chukchi people 10, 12
creation myths 6, 8–9, 14–15, 25, 26, 29, 30, 54, 56, 64

Cuchulain 26, 38
Cupid 42, 46, 67
Cyclopes 16, 26, 27
Damayanti 35
death 7, 23, 28, 29, 33, 56, 58–59, 67, 69
Dekanah-wida 32
Delphi, oracle at 40, 64, 66
Demeter 7, 24, 66
Diana 12, 37
Dionysus 45, 66, 67
Dogon people 10, 26, 58
dragons 16, 30, 32, 50–51, 66, 68
Dreamtime 6, 7, 29, 35, 54, 56, 61
Druids 60, 67
Durga 31

EF

Ea 13, 16
Earth 11, 20; as mother goddess 6, 11, 20, 21, 22, 24–25, 64
Easter Island see Rapa Nui
egg, cosmic 6, 8, 10, 15
Egypt, ancient 6, 11, 12, 13, 24, 25, 26, 28, 45, 58, 62, 63, 66, 67, 69; animal gods 6, 48, 56, 57; creation myths 8, 14, 15; pyramids 60, 65
Epona 24
Eshu 6, 36, 40, 44–45
Ewe people 42
Fafnir 32, 50
Fenrir 26, 63
fertility deities 6, 13, 23, 24–25
Flora 23
Fortuna 42
Frey and Freya 24, 36, 39
Fuji, Mount 19, 60

GHI

Gaia 8
Galahad, Sir 35
Ganesha 39, 40
Garuda 7, 49
Geb 11
Gesar 32
Ghede 58
Gilgamesh 13, 18, 33, 48, 65
Golden Fleece 34
Gorgons 51
Greeks, ancient 7, 8, 19, 21, 22, 24, 25, 26, 33, 38, 40, 42, 59, 61, 65; beasts 50, 51, 64; flood myths 18, 19; heroes 16, 26, 32, 33, 34, 36;

Greeks, ancient contd.
plant lore 66, 67;
see also Zeus
Gu 38
Guan Di 6, 39
Hathor 18
heaven 33, 39, 59, 60
Hel 26, 30
hell 59
Hera 16, 25, 26, 65, 66
Heracles 16, 26, 36, 50, 66, 67
Hermes 16
Hiawatha 32
Hinduism 7, 18, 20, 26, 32, 49, 54, 62, 66; creation myths 6, 9, 14, 54, 56; evil beings 30, 31, 39; see also Vishnu
Hiranyakashipu 46
Hittites 24
Ho-Ho twins 42–43
Holy Grail 35
Horus 13, 25, 26, 58
Huldufolk 46
Hunahpu 30, 58
Inari 22, 48
Incas 13, 19, 24, 61
Inti 13, 61
Inuits 10, 12, 14, 22, 23
Ireland 26, 38, 64
Ishtar 11, 13, 25, 33, 38
Isis 6, 25, 26
Izanagi 9, 21, 31

JKL

Jade Emperor 17
Japan 7, 9, 10, 13, 18, 19, 21, 22, 28, 29, 31, 40, 42, 43, 45, 60, 66, 67
Jason and the Argonauts 34, 67, 68
Kasyapa 48, 49
Kathakali dance 54
Kelpie 53
Khnum 15
Kitsune 52
Kraken 47
Krishna 11, 32, 66
Ku 38
Kusa-nada-hime 31
Kwan-non 43
Loki 26, 30, 44
Lone Man 8, 18
Louhi 17
love 11, 25, 42–43, 67

MNO

Manu 18, 26
Māoris 11, 21, 23, 56

Marduk 16
Maui-Of-A-Thousand-Tricks 45
Mawu-Lisa 14, 16, 38
Maya 19, 30, 57, 58, 64, 65
Medusa 33, 38, 51
Mesopotamia 18, 33, 38
Mexico 24, 59, 64, 65; see also Aztecs; Maya
Mictlantecuhtli 16, 59
Minotaur 33
Monkey King 53
monsters 26, 27, 30, 33, 50–51, 57, 64
Moon 11, 12–13, 26, 30, 31, 33, 60
Morrigan 38
mother goddess 6, 11, 20, 21, 22, 24–25
nagas 48
Nala 35
Namarrgon 21
Nana-Buluku 16
Native Americans 8, 12, 13, 18, 24–25, 32, 36, 40, 43, 44, 50, 54, 55, 56, 62, 63, 66; creation myths 8, 9, 56, 64; rituals and art 41, 54–55; totem poles 60–61
Ngolimeno 42
Nisse 47
Noah 19
Nommo 26
Norse myths 7, 14, 24, 26, 30, 32, 36–37, 39, 44, 50, 63, 64, 66; see also Odin; Vikings
Nut 11, 12
Nyame 16, 17, 44
Oceania 23, 36
Odin 14, 26, 30, 36, 37, 38, 39, 63
Odysseus 21, 27, 34
Ogun 37
Olokun 20
Olympus, Mount 16
One Thousand and One Nights 35
Oshun 28
Osiris 24, 26, 34, 48, 57, 58, 66, 67

PQR

Pacha Mama 24
Pan 22, 48
Pan Gu 10
Papua New Guinea 28–29, 56
Paracas people 55
Pegasus 50, 51

Pele 20
Persephone 7, 24, 67
Perseus 16, 33
Persians 8
pipes of peace 41
planets 8–9, 65
Polynesia 7, 10, 14–15, 21, 45
Poseidon 19, 21, 26, 27, 33, 67, 68
Prometheus 18
pyramids 60, 65
Quetzalcoatl 6, 16, 48, 65
Ra 13, 14, 25, 48, 60, 62, 63
Ragnarok 59, 63
Rainbow Snake 34, 35
Rapa Nui (Easter Island) 8, 29, 69
Romans 7, 12, 23, 25, 28, 38, 42, 45, 65, 66, 67
Romulus and Remus 28, 66
Rübezahl 47

ST

sacrifices 22, 31, 40
sand-paintings 54, 55
Sedna 10, 22, 23
Sekhmet 6, 48, 69
Selkie 52
shamans 6–7, 12, 17, 40, 41, 65
Shamash 11, 13, 48
Shango 28, 36, 54
Shiva 40, 54
Sigurd 32
Sinbad 35
Sirens 34
Skanda 39
sky deities 11, 12, 16, 17, 20–21
snake dance 54
Sobek 48, 57
Solar System 8–9, 65
Sphinx 64
spring deities 22, 23
Stonehenge 60
stones, standing 69
storms 16, 18–19, 21, 31, 36
storytelling 7, 54
Sun 12–13, 26, 30, 31, 33, 36, 45, 48, 49, 60, 61, 62, 63
Sun Dance 41
Susano 13, 31, 45
Tane 11, 23, 36
Tangaroa 7, 14–15, 36
Taoism 17, 66
Tawhaki 21
Tengu 45
Theseus 33
Thor 7, 37
Thoth 12, 25

thunder and lightning 21, 28, 36, 37, 54, 60
Thunderbird 36, 60–61
Tiamat 16
Tibet 30, 32, 36–37
Tiv 40
Toci 21
torii 60
Tristan and Isolde 50
trolls 46
Tupan 36, 65
turtles 9, 26, 56
twins 8, 26, 30, 36, 42–43, 58

UVW

Ulgan and Erlik 30
Uluru (Ayers Rock) 61
underworld 26, 30, 33, 34, 58–59, 62, 67
unicorns 50, 51
Utnapishtim 18
Väinämöinen 17
Vajrapani 30
vajras 30, 36–37
Valkyries and Valhalla 39, 59
vampires 53
Venus 25, 42, 65, 67
Vikings 8, 10, 37, 40, 59, 63, 66; see also Norse myths
Viracocha 13
Vishnu 9, 10–11, 18, 26, 32, 46, 49, 56, 62
voodoo 40, 58
Vucub-Caquix 30
wampum 32
war deities 7, 11, 21, 28, 31, 37, 38–39
water deities 13, 20, 24, 26, 28; see also Poseidon; Tangaroa
waves, giant 18–19, 36
werewolves 53
Willendorf goddess 25
witches 30
wolves 26, 28, 53, 63

XYZ

Xbalanque 30, 58
Xipe Totec 22
Yen-lo 58
Yggdrasil 10, 66
Yi 33
yin and yang 10
Yoruba people 28, 36, 37, 40, 44, 54
Zeus 7, 16, 18, 20, 26, 33, 36, 38, 48, 59, 65

Acknowledgements

Dorling Kindersley would like to thank: Akan Hills, Philip Nicholls, Christi Graham, John Williams, Kevin Lovelock, Jim Rossiter, and Janet Peckham of the British Museum, London; Kalamandalam Vijayakumar and Kalamandalam Barbara Vijayakumar; and the African Crafts Centre, Covent Garden, London.
Photography: Andy Crawford; **Researcher:** Robert Graham; **Index:** Chris Bernstein; **Design assistance:** Jill Bunyan and Anna Martin; **Proofreading:** Sarah Owens; **Wallchart:** Peter Radcliffe, Steve Setford; **Clipart CD:** Jo Little, Claire Watts, Jessamy Wood; Andrea Mills for editing the relaunch version and Victoria Pyke for proofreading it.

The publishers would like to thank the following for their kind permission to reproduce their photographs:

Picture Credits (Key: a-above; b-below/bottom; c-centre; f-far; l-left; r-right; t-top)

AKG Images: 39tr, 39l, Boymans van Beuningen Museum, Rotterdam *The Tower of Babel*, Pieter Brueghel the Elder 7r; Erich Lessing/ Württembergisches Landesmuseum, Stuttgart 7bcr, 24tl, 48tl; SMPK Kupferstichkabinett, Berlin 12tl; Torquil Cramer 62/63c; Universitets Oldsaksamling, Oslo 32bc; Von der Heydt Museum, Wuppertal Flora, *Awakening Flowers*, 1876, by Arnold Bucklin (1827–1901) 23bl; **Alamy Stock Photo:** AF archive 53c, age fotostock 52bl, Classic Image 35tl, David Robertson 53r, Dinodia Photos 46crb, Granger Historical Picture Archive 53br, imageBROKER 47bl, Ivy Close Images 34crb, Jeffrey Thompson 52tl, Julie Quarry 46cra, Ken Cavanagh 46bl, Mary Evans Picture Library 34cr, 47tr, 47cla, Michel & Gabrielle Therin-Weise 52cl,

Peter Barritt 34l, TAO Images Limited 52-53b, United Archives GmbH 35tr, 35clb; **American Museum of Natural History:** 43br, 54tr, 56cl; Thos. Beiswenger 41r; **Ancient Art & Architecture Collection:** 64tl; D.F. Head 29tr; Ronald Sheridan 8bl, 11br, 21d, 24br, 25ar, 45l, 45ca; **The Art Archive:** Buonconsiglio Castle Trento/Dagli Orti 66cr; Musée du Louvre Paris/Dagli Orti 69br; National Gallery London/Eileen Tweedy 69c; Dagli Orti 65bc, 66bc; Mireille Vautier 44tl; **Ashmolean Museum,** Oxford: 14c, 30br, 42/43c; **Duncan Baird Publishers Archive:** 14tl; Japanese Gallery 9cr, 31c; **Bildarchiv Preußisches Kulturbesitz:** 32tl; SMPK Berlin 16; Staatliche Museum, Berlin 50tr; **Bridgeman Art Library, London/New York:** British Museum, London *The Weighing of the Heart Against Maat's Feather of Truth,* Egyptian, early 19th Dynasty, c.1300 BCE, Book of the Dead of the Royal Scribe 58br; By Courtesy of the Board of the Trustees of the V&A *Vishnu in the Centre of his Ten Avatars,* Jaipur area, 18th century 18tl; Galleria degli Uffizi, Florence, Italy *The Birth of Venus,* c.1485, by Sandro Botticelli (1444/5–1510) 42cl; Louvre, Paris, France/Giraudon *Stele of a Woman before Re- Harakhy,* Egyptian, c.1000BC 13tl; Musée Condé, Chantilly, France MS 860/421 f.7 *The Story of Adam and Eve,* detail from "Cas des Nobles Homimes et Femmes" by Boccaccio, translated by Laurent de Premierfait, French 1465, *Works of Giovanni Boccaccio* (1313–75) 7bl (right), 15br; Museo Correr, Venice, Italy *Glimpse of Hell* (panel) by Flemish School (15th century) 59bl; Piazza della Signoria, Florence/Lauros - Giraudon *Perseus with the Head of a Medusa,* 1545–1554, in the Loggia dei Lanzi, by Benvenuto Cellini (1500–1571) 33bcr; Private Collection Genesis 6:11–24 Noah's Ark, Nuremberg Bible (Biblia Sacra Germanaica), 1483 19bc; **Bridgeman Images:** 35b; **British Museum, London:** 4br, 4bl, 7bc, 11tr, 12tr,

14r, 15c, 15r, 15r, 15tr, 17r, 21t, 23tl, 26bl, 29br, 33 tr, 36c, 38br, 39bc, 42tl, 43tc, 43tr, 56bl, 57tl; **Cambridge Museum of Anthropology:** 19r, 61tr; **Central Art Archives:** The Old Students House, Helsinki 17tl; **Dreamstime.com:** Alexander Makatserchyk 47br; **Jean-Loup Charmet:** 7tr, 19tl; **Christie's Images:** *In the Well of the Great Wave of Kanagawa,* c.1797, by Hokusai Katsushika (1760–1849) 18/19b, 28r, 29l; **Bruce Coleman Ltd:** Jeff Foott Productions 41tl; Chinch Gryniewicz/ Ecoscene 66–67; Michael S. Yamashita 68–69; **CM Dixon:** 29bc; **DK Picture Library:** American Museum of Natural History/Lynton Gardiner 71tc; British Museum 70tr; Glasgow Museum 70tcl; INAH/Michel Zabé 71bl; Statens Historika Museum, Stockholm 71bl; **Edimedia:** 12cr; **E.T. Archive:** 31l; British Library Or 13805 60bl; Freer Gallery of Art 22br; Victoria & Albert Museum, London 10/11c; **Mary Evans Picture Library:** 10bl, 10br, 21bl, 26c, 28tl, 30bl; **Werner Forman Archive:** Anthropology Museum, Veracruz University, Jalapa 59r; Arhus Kunstmuseum, Denmark 30cl; Dallas Museum of Art 26bl; David Bernstein Fine Art, New York 55r; Field Museum of Natural History, Chicago 9t; Museum of the American Indian, Heye Foundation 13cl; Smithsonian Institution 12cl; State Museum of Berlin 16cl; **Glasgow Museums (St Mungo):** 31bl, 32bl, 40bl, 54br, 58tr; **Ronald Grant Archive:** Columbia Pictures 68bc; **Hamburgisches Museum für Völkerkunde:** 45tr; **Robert Harding Picture Library:** Patrick Mathews 56bl; **Heritage Image Partnership:** James Sowerby 67cla; **Michael Holford:** British Museum 7cr (below), 8bc, 8tl, 13bl, 14bl, 42bl, 61cr; Kunisada 13br; Museum of Mankind 44bl; Victoria & Albert Museum, London 9br; **Hutchison Library:** Ian Lloyd 63br; **INAH/Michael Zabe:** 19tc, 22l, 16bc; **Barnabas Kindersley:** 59tl, 59ca; **Lonely Planet Images:** George Tsafos 8tr; **MacQuitty International Photo Collection:** 41bl; **Nilesh Mistry:** 30tl; **Musée de L'Homme, France:** 20l; D Ponsard 38l, 60tl; **Museum of Anthropology,**

Vancouver: 63cl; **Museum of Mankind:** 4cl, 32c, 37tc; **NASA:** 65cl; **National Maritime Museum:** 2c, 51tr; **National Museum of Copenhagen:** 36/37b; **The Board of Trustees of the National Museums & Galleries on Merseyside:** 28bl, 57tr; **Natural History Museum, London:** 2tcl, 27tr, 27c, 50/51b, 50tl, 51tl, 51r, 70bl; © David Neel, 1998: 2tl; **Peter Newark's Pictures:** 16r, 41cl, 55c; **Panos Pictures:** Caroline Penn 63bl; **Ann & Bury Peerless:** 20cl, 49tl; **Pitt Rivers Museum, Oxford:** 6bcl, 10tr, 23cr, 40tr 57bl; Zither 17tc; **Planet Earth Pictures:** Jan Tove Johansson 8l; **Axel Poignant Archive:** 11cl, 21fr, 37tl; **Rex Features:** Tim Brooke 59bcl; **Rijksmuiseum voor Volkenkunde:** 20r; **Réunion des Musées Nationaux Agence Photographique:** Hervé Lewandowski 26tl, 33cr; Richard Lambert 39cr; **Royal Ontario Museum:** 67tr; **Science Photo Library:** Chris Bjornberg 8/9c; Sally Benusen (1982) 60/61c; **South American Pictures:** Tony Morrison 13tr, 62cr; **Spectrum Colour Library:** 62cr; Statens Historika Museum, Stockholm: 9br; Oliver Strewe: 29cra; **Topham Picturepoint:** 64cr, 65cra, 69tl; **123RF. com:** Amnart Suwannakan 46tl, panda3800 53cb.

Wallchart: Alamy Images: Ancient Art & Architecture Collection Ltd cra (ishtar); Image Gap bl; **Dorling Kindersley:** Courtesy of The American Museum of Natural History cl (Shaman mask); Courtesy of the Manchester Museum clb (Aphrodite); Courtesy of the National Museum, New Delhi cr (Durga); Courtesy of the Royal Ontario Museum, Toronto tl; Courtesy of the University Museum of Archaeology and Anthropology, Cambridge fbr; James McConnachie / Rough Guides bc (Chimera); Rob Reichenfeld / Courtesy of Bishop's Museum, Hawaii crb (Ku War God); **Getty Images:** Guy Edwardes / Photographer's Choice ftl; Robert Harding br (Dogon); Jeremy Woodhouse / Photodisc crb (coyote); **Photolibrary:** Brand X Pictures fbr (skull).

All other images © Dorling Kindersley
For further information, see: **www.dkimages.com**